WILD TURKEY KITCHEN

CELEBRATIONS BIG AND SMALL

Betsy Doty

Copyright © 2021 by Betsy Doty

All rights reserved. No part of this publication may be reproduced, distributed or transmitted in any form or by any means, including photocopying, recording, or other electronic or mechanical methods, without the prior written permission of the publisher, except in the case of brief quotations embodied in critical reviews and certain other noncommercial uses permitted by copyright law.

Wild Turkey Kitchen/Betsy Doty —1st ed.

Cover Design by Liliana Guia
Editing by Jessica Easto

ISBN 978-1-943658-76-3 (paperback)
ISBN 978-1-943658-77-0 (hardback)

Treaty Oak Publishers

For Gordon, Eric, and Neal

CONTENTS

Author's Note 14
Introduction 17
Equipment Notes 18

SUNDAY DINNER   21

Wild Turkey Lemonade 22
Bourbon Meatloaf 24
Herbed Polenta With Brie 27
Roasted Potatoes 28
Asian-Style Tomato Salad 29
Shaved Brussels Sprouts Salad 30
Flan 33

WINE TASTING PARTY   35

Spanakopita 36
Sun-Dried Tomato Dip on Pringles 39
Bacon and Pecan Pimento Cheese 40
Mango Guacamole Dip 43
Flourless Orange and Almond Cookies 44
Chocolate-Truffle Cookies 47

BIRTHDAY CELEBRATION   49

Cheese Böreks 50
Chicken Paprikas 52

Contents

Vegetable Toss	54
Provincial Cherry Tomato Gratin	55
Mexican Chocolate Pepita Cake with Candied Ancho Chiles	56

    Chocolate Ganache 59
    Raspberry Sauce 60
    Vanilla Custard Sauce 61

Awesome Coconut Cake	62

    Coconut Cream Cheese Frosting 63

BUNCO PARTY OR DINNER FOR TWELVE   65

Candied Bacon Bites	66
Chicken Vegetable Cobbler	69
Waldorf Salad	73
Sweet and Spicy Candied Pecans	74
Fresh Tomato and Cucumber Salad	75
Lemon Cake	76

    Lemon Cream Cheese Glaze 77

Dark Chocolate Pudding with Toasted Coconut	78

BABY LIT SHOWER   81

Ginger Grapefruit Sparklers	82
Peppermint Cranberry Mocktails	82
Red Fish, Blue Fish, Tuna Salad	84
Mad Hatter Cucumber Tea Sandwiches	85
Deviled Green Eggs and Ham	87
Mr. McGregor's Cakes (The World's Best Carrot Cake)	88

    Cream Cheese Frosting 91

In the Night Kitchen Bourbon Pecan Cookies	93

Contents

BACKYARD GRILL — **95**

Summer Bourbon Rickey 97
Naan 98
Beef Sliders with Sweet and Sour Red Onions 100
Chicken Tikka Skewers 103
Watermelon Chaat 104
Cucumber Raita 105
Lemon Jasmine Rice Salad 106
Charlie Bird's Farro Salad 107
Frozen Lime Pie 109
Banana Cream Pudding 110
    Vanilla Pastry Cream 112
    Marshmallow Meringue 113

BOOK CLUB — **115**

Brisket on a Biscuit 116
Tomato Bisque 118
Spicy Cold Tomato Soup 120
Cowboy Caviar 123
Mixed Fruit Crisp with Almonds 124
Midnight Chocolate Cake with Orange-Lemon Curd Filling . . 126
    Orange-Lemon Curd Filling 127
    Sugared Pecans 129

CHRISTMAS EVE — **131**

Barcelona Sangria 132
Mexican-Style Meatball Soup 134
Bibb Lettuce and Orange Salad 136

Contents

Bourbon Walnut Pie 138

Oma's Molasses Cookies 140

NEW YEAR'S EVE   143

Americano Cocktail 144

Italian Skewers 145

Pear and Walnut Salad 146

Boeuf Bourguignon 147

Parslied Potatoes 150

Green Peas with Parmesan 151

Almond Cream Pie 152

Amaretto Cream Cake with Raspberry Filling 154
    Italian Cream Cheese Frosting   156
    Raspberry Filling   157

BREAKFAST WITH FRIENDS   159

Citrus Medley 160

Fruit with Yogurt and Granola 161

Huevos Rancheros 162

Banana and Date Muffins 165

Pfannkuchen 166

Apple Compote 168

Crunchy Granola 169

Index 170

DRINKS

Americano Cocktail	144
Barcelona Sangria	132
Ginger Grapefruit Sparklers	82
Peppermint Cranberry Mocktails	82
Summer Bourbon Rickey	97
Wild Turkey Lemonade	22

APPETIZERS

Bacon and Pecan Pimento Cheese	40
Candied Bacon Bites	66
Cheese Böreks	50
Cowboy Caviar	123
Deviled Green Eggs and Ham	87
Italian Skewers	145
Mad Hatter Cucumber Tea Sandwiches	85
Mango Guacamole Dip	43
Spanakopita	36
Sun-Dried Tomato Dip on Pringles	39

SOUPS

MEXICAN-STYLE MEATBALL SOUP	134
SPICY COLD TOMATO SOUP	120
TOMATO BISQUE	118

MAINS

BOURBON MEATLOAF	24
CHICKEN PAPRIKAS	52
CHICKEN VEGETABLE COBBLER	69
BEEF SLIDERS WITH SWEET AND SOUR RED ONIONS	100
CHICKEN TIKKA SKEWERS	103
BRISKET ON A BISCUIT	116
BOEUF BOURGUIGNON	147

Contents

SALADS & SIDES

Asian-Style Tomato Salad	29
Bibb Lettuce and Orange Salad	136
Charlie Bird's Farro Salad	107
Cucumber Raita	105
Fresh Tomato and Cucumber Salad	75
Green Peas with Parmesan	151
Herbed Polenta With Brie	27
Lemon Jasmine Rice Salad	106
Naan	98
Parslied Potatoes	150
Pear and Walnut Salad	146
Provincial Cherry Tomato Gratin	55
Red Fish, Blue Fish, Tuna Salad	84
Roasted Potatoes	28
Shaved Brussels Sprouts Salad	30
Sweet and Spicy Candied Pecans	74
Vegetable Toss	54
Waldorf Salad	73
Watermelon Chaat	104

Contents

DESSERTS

Almond Cream Pie 152

Amaretto Cream Cake with Raspberry Filling . . . 154
    Italian Cream Cheese Frosting 156
    Raspberry Filling 157

Awesome Coconut Cake 62
    Coconut Cream Cheese Frosting 63

Banana Cream Pudding 110
    Marshmallow Meringue 113
    Vanilla Pastry Cream 112

Bourbon Walnut Pie 138

Chocolate-Truffle Cookies 47

Dark Chocolate Pudding with Toasted Coconut . . . 78

Flan 33

Flourless Orange and Almond Cookies 44

Frozen Lime Pie. 109

In the Night Kitchen Bourbon Pecan Cookies 93

Lemon Cake. 76
    Lemon Cream Cheese Glaze 77

Mexican Chocolate Pepita Cake with Candied Ancho Chiles . . . 56
    Chocolate Ganache 59
    Raspberry Sauce 60
    Vanilla Custard Sauce 61

Midnight Chocolate Cake with Orange-Lemon Curd Filling . . . 126
    Orange-Lemon Curd Filling 127
    Sugared Pecans 129

Mixed Fruit Crisp with Almonds 124

Mr. McGregor's Cakes (The World's Best Carrot Cake). . . 88
    Cream Cheese Frosting 91

Oma's Molasses Cookies. 140

Contents

BREAKFAST & BRUNCH

Apple Compote 168

Banana and Date Muffins 165

Citrus Medley 160

Crunchy Granola 169

Fruit with Yogurt and Granola 161

Huevos Rancheros 162

Pfannkuchen 166

Author's Note

This book started as a retirement project and a way to document family recipes for my sons. As I began to write, cook, and experiment with menus and recipes, the audience expanded as did the scope of the book. My testers reinforced the strength of the recipes, and with every celebratory meal, my confidence increased.

You'll see mention of Fran Woodfin throughout this book. She is my older sister and an excellent creative cook. We share recipes frequently, and throughout the years, she was the one who documented and experimented with our family recipes. She has impeccable taste, and I highly value her opinion and thank both her and her husband, Bill, for all their recipe testing. My husband, Charles, was my initial editor and cheerleader. His encouragement and patience with all the dirty dishes played an integral role in the completion of this project.

In year two of writing this book, the COVID-19 virus struck. Suddenly the premise of this book, "Celebrations, Big and Small," evaporated. I no longer could host dinner parties for our friends, birthday celebrations were severely limited, and our socializing revolved around food-free Zoom chats. This seemed like the last kind of cookbook anyone wanted, much less needed. But we humans are optimistic; I pushed on and shared my cooking experiments mostly with my husband and my freezer and with a few willing neighbors.

Eventually, I figured out how to host a Zoom wine tasting party by preparing individual appetizer bags for pickup.

Author's Note

For my husband's birthday party, I boxed individual carrot cupcakes and shared them under the canopy of Live Oaks in our neighbor's yard.

In the summer, our neighbors set up an outdoor movie theater with their house foundation as the screen. I gingerly passed out whatever the sweet concoction was for the week. The need for celebrations with food and drink never diminished, even though the execution stretched my imagination.

Cooking began for me at an early age as a form of entertainment and a way to fight off boredom. Home alone during the summer while my parents worked, I was old enough to strike a match to light our 1950s gas oven, but not tall enough to reach the upper shelves of the cabinets. My mother's only cookbook was the iconic red and white plaid–covered *Better Homes and Gardens New Cook Book*. Like a chicken scratching for food, I paged relentlessly through her cookbook, hunting for dessert recipes that contained ingredients found in our pantry.

Taffy is made from only a few ingredients (sugar, vanilla, and butter), and everything was available in our kitchen. As with most recipes of few ingredients, success was all about the technique.

Boil the sugar and water until reaching the hard boil stage. Drop a teaspoon of the mixture into a glass of water to test the stage. Pour out the hot mixture and pull.

Author's Note

Ignorance has its benefits. I didn't realize that, for a nine-year-old, this was advanced cooking. Many times, I carefully watched the blob of sugar and water coagulate and float to the top of the glass, but I was never successful in creating the soft, creamy candy of my imagination. Instead, my labors produced a jawbreaking mound of hard sugar.

Next, I moved on to lemon pie, another failure. I didn't have the vegetable shortening that was called for in the crust, so I substituted Wesson cooking oil, big mistake. The filling was marginal, but the crust was raw and inedible. Later, I attempted baking cakes and managed to produce something that was slightly better than a hockey puck. Eventually through trial and error, my baking improved, and I was designated the family cake baker.

I didn't expand beyond desserts until I moved to my first apartment during my senior year of college. Not only did I have my own kitchen but I had the very real need to eat. Luckily, my roommate was an excellent cook, and her recipe repertoire far exceeded mine. During my first visit home at Thanksgiving, I filled note cards with recipes my mother dictated: tuna salad, tacos, rice, beans, potato salad, spaghetti sauce. These formulas could sustain me. I still have those note cards and though my spaghetti sauce has evolved, her tuna salad remains a staple in our house.

This book is a mixture of family recipes shared throughout the generations, my own original creations, and many tried-and-true chef-created dishes.

My three sons have become cooks in their own right. I can't say they grew up eating delicious creative dishes. No, daily lunch was peanut butter and jelly sandwiches, and their favorite meal was boxed macaroni and cheese and jarred applesauce, my attempt at a balanced meal. This book is for them.

Introduction

Our days are bookended by weekends and our years by holidays and special occasions. Celebrating these occasions with delightful meals shared among family and friends inspired the format for this book. For me, the menu planning, be it a simple Sunday dinner or an elaborate Christmas meal, is where the real enjoyment begins. Whether you're an experienced cook or only grace the kitchen for special occasions, preparing delicious menus, hot and on time without your nerves frayed or your kitchen a disaster, is the goal of this book.

Each chapter contains a celebration, big or small, with complete menus and recipes. Make-ahead options are there to help with the daunting prospect of putting a complete dinner on the table. These menus should be a jumping off point for your own creativity; prepare the entire meal, or pick and choose a single recipe. Come join me now inside my Texas hill country kitchen, on the intoxicating street Wild Turkey Pass.

Equipment Notes

BAKING SHEET

The term "baking sheet" refers to both cookie sheets and rimmed half-sheet pans (18 inches by 13 inches). The difference being that a cookie sheet will only have one or two raised edges so that the cookies can slide off the sides easily. Either kind of pan can be used for cookies. When a raised edge is needed in a recipe, it is specified.

CAKE PANS

I use aluminized steel baking pans and always grease them with butter or pan spray, dust with flour, and place parchment on the bottom to further prevent sticking. The parchment paper seems redundant, but it's worth the extra effort. It's disheartening to see your beautifully baked cake stuck to the bottom of the pan.

DIGITAL THERMOMETER

My roasting skills improved immensely when I added a leave-in oven probe thermometer to my kitchen arsenal. That and my instant-read thermometer, which I refer to as "digital thermometers", are worth every penny paid for them. Having said that, I only call for a digital thermometer in the Equipment section when I think it is essential for your success.

ELECTRIC MIXER

My stand mixer is an essential part of my kitchen, and I can't imagine baking without it. I do use an electric hand-held mixer when beating small quantities or if the stand mixer is in use. I realize that not everyone needs or wants another appliance, so even though the mixing may be more tedious, the recipes in this book can be made using a hand-held mixer. I note in the Equipment section when a stand mixer is most important.

PIE PLATES

I use either inexpensive glass or metal pie plates. They seem to be the best for even browning. I've largely abandoned any fancy decorative ceramic pie plates and let the beauty of the crisp crust stand for itself.

WIRE RACK

A grid patterned wire cooling rack is one of my most used kitchen tools. It not only prevents soggy bottoms from baked goods but also substitutes as a roasting rack when set inside a rimmed baking sheet. I only call it out in the Equipment section when it is used for roasting.

Wild Turkey Lemonade

Bourbon Meatloaf

Herbed Polenta with Brie
or
Roasted Potatoes

Asian-Style Tomato Salad

Shaved Brussels Sprouts Salad

Flan

Make Ahead
Up to 3 weeks before: Make the simple syrup for the lemonade.
Day before: Make the flan and the Brussels sprouts salad.
Early in the day: Make the dressing for the tomato salad, mix the meatloaf, cover, and refrigerate.
Last hour: Prepare the potatoes or cook the polenta, bake the meatloaf, mix together the tomato salad.

SUNDAY DINNER

While growing up, our family always ate dinner together, a rarity in many households today. No matter how informal the meal or how tired my mother was from her accounting job at the Texas Highway Department, she always prepared a meat, vegetable, and starch. These were quick, simple meals. Often the salad, served on its own plate, was iceberg lettuce with a canned pear, a dollop of Hellmann's mayonnaise, and a sprinkling of cheddar cheese. I thought everyone ate this way.

During the week, we sat at a modest metal folding table in the kitchen. It was covered with a cheerful red-and-white checked tablecloth and set with fork, knife, and napkin. Above our heads, an open shelf displayed a Bavarian beer stein and German Hummels from my parent's tour in Germany. On Sundays and when there were visitors, my mother served dinner in our small dining room. My grandmother's hand-crocheted place mats protected the polished wood table, and my mother's wedding silverware graced each place setting.

This is a simple cocktail with fresh ingredients that highlight the bourbon. The plain soda cuts the alcohol and adds a bit of fizz. Serve it alongside a handful of salted nuts while the family awaits the meatloaf.

WILD TURKEY LEMONADE

SERVES 1 | EQUIPMENT: Collins glass

2 ounces bourbon or rye

1 ounce simple syrup

1 ounce fresh lemon juice

Soda, for topping

1 lemon slice, for garnish

Fresh mint, for garnish (optional)

1. Combine the bourbon, simple syrup, and lemon juice.
2. Pour into an ice-filled Collins glass and top with soda. Garnish with a lemon slice and fresh mint (if using).

To make the simple syrup, mix one part sugar to one part water and heat to combine. Once the sugar is dissolved, let the sugar mixture cool and store in the refrigerator for up to three weeks.

Sunday Dinner

Meatloaf has a bad rap with some people. I'm not sure why: it's inexpensive, nutritious, and delicious—perfect for an informal Sunday dinner. This recipe serves four generously but can be doubled or stretched if your family is larger.

Inspiration for the techniques and some of the ingredients came from a 2017 Wall Street Journal *recipe by chef Edward Lee. The addition of pecans to the mixture is a nod to my Texas heritage and was a staple in my mother's meatloaf.*

This recipe does not call for a loaf pan. Instead, mold the meat mixture in a free-form manner to resemble a traditional meatloaf and place it atop a wire rack inside a rimmed baking sheet. The result is a quicker cooking and moister loaf. I use a meat thermometer to ensure doneness.

BOURBON MEATLOAF

SERVES 4 | EQUIPMENT: wire rack, pastry brush

- 1 tablespoon unsalted butter
- 1 cup finely chopped onion
- 1 cup diced red bell pepper
- ½ cup finely chopped celery
- 1 garlic clove, minced
- 3 ounces bacon, cut into 1¼-inch dice (3 or 4 slices)
- 1 pound 80% lean ground chuck beef
- ½ cup bread crumbs (Panko is a good choice)
- ½ cup chopped pecans
- 1 large egg, lightly beaten
- ½ cup ketchup plus 1 tablespoon (divided)
- 1½ tablespoons bourbon
- 1 tablespoon Worcestershire sauce
- 1 teaspoon kosher salt
- ½ teaspoon ground black pepper
- ½ tablespoon soy sauce
- ½ teaspoon sriracha, or more as needed

1. Preheat the oven to 375°F. Line a rimmed baking sheet with parchment paper or aluminum foil (for easy cleanup) and place a wire rack on top. Cover the wire rack with aluminum foil or parchment paper.

2. In a large skillet over medium heat, melt the butter. Add the onion, bell pepper, celery, and garlic. Sauté until the onions are translucent, about 3 minutes. Stir in the bacon and sauté until the bacon lightly browns, about 6 minutes.

3   Transfer the onion mixture to a large bowl and let cool slightly. Add the ground beef, bread crumbs, pecans, egg, ¼ cup of the ketchup, the bourbon, Worcestershire sauce, salt, and pepper. With clean hands, mix everything together until the ingredients are evenly distributed. Do not pack down; use a light hand when mixing.

4   Transfer the meat mixture to the prepared wire rack and pat into a loaf that is about 2½ inches high. *Note: The meatloaf can be made ahead, covered, and placed in the refrigerator until 30 minutes before baking.*

5   Prepare the glaze. In a small bowl, mix the remaining ¼ cup plus 1 tablespoon of ketchup with the soy sauce and sriracha until well combined.

6   Bake the meatloaf for 10 minutes, then remove it from the oven and brush the glaze over the top. Return the meatloaf to the oven and bake until it is just cooked through and the internal temperature reads 145°F to 150°F on a meat thermometer, about 40 minutes more. Remove from the oven and let it cool slightly before serving.

Serve this dish when you want the creaminess of mashed potatoes without the fuss of peeling and mashing potatoes. Polenta, made from ground yellow corn, is the Italian equivalent to Southern grits, which is made from white corn and has a coarser grind. To me, polenta is also more complex in flavor.

The inspiration to add herbes de Provence and Brie cheese to polenta came from the Savory Spice Test Kitchen. The blend is a refreshing change to the standard grits and cheddar that is so popular on Southern tables.

The herbes de Provence mixture consists of thyme, marjoram, summer savory, rosemary, tarragon, basil, fennel seeds, mint, chervil, and lavender. If you don't want to use this blend, substitute your favorite herbs, and if you prefer something more traditional, grated cheddar cheese never fails.

HERBED POLENTA WITH BRIE

SERVES 4 to 6

- 2 cups whole or 2% milk
- 2 cups water
- 1 cup polenta
- 1 tablespoon herbes de Provence
- 1 teaspoon sea salt
- Pinch ground black pepper
- 4 ounce Brie cheese, rind removed and diced
- 3 tablespoons unsalted butter, room temperature
- ¼ cup roasted and salted pumpkin seeds (optional)

1. Bring the milk and water to a boil in a medium saucepan over medium-high heat. Slowly stir in the polenta.
2. Reduce the heat to low and simmer while adding the herbes de Provence, salt, and pepper. Cook for about 10 minutes, stirring frequently, until thick and creamy.
3. Remove from the heat and stir in the cheese and butter. Top with the pumpkin seeds (if using) and serve.

Roasted potatoes go well with the meatloaf and can share the oven space. These potatoes are good on their own or can be spiced with the addition of garlic and herbs at the end of cooking.

ROASTED POTATOES

SERVES 4

8 small red or white potatoes, unpeeled (about 1½ pounds)
2 tablespoons extra-virgin olive oil
¾ teaspoon kosher salt
½ teaspoon ground black pepper

1. Preheat the oven to 375°F.
2. Cut the potatoes in half or quarters so they are roughly all the same size.
3. In a medium bowl, toss the potatoes with the oil, salt, and pepper.
4. Pour them onto a rimmed baking sheet and spread into a single layer.
5. Bake for about 50 minutes, tossing halfway through to ensure even browning. The potatoes should be crisp on the outside and easily pierced with a fork.

The cooking time varies depending on the size of your potatoes.

Sliced fresh summertime tomatoes with a bit of salt and pepper are a perfect accompaniment to meatloaf or any summer dinner, for that matter. When you don't have the luxury of homegrown or farmers market tomatoes, the spices in this salad make up for less-than-stellar tomatoes. Melissa Clark's Weeknight Kitchen *podcast inspired this adaptation.*

I've learned that when adding raw garlic to salads, using a Microplane to grate the garlic is the easiest method for even distribution. Of course, you can always mince if you want to save on washing.

ASIAN-STYLE TOMATO SALAD

SERVES 4 | EQUIPMENT: Microplane

- 1 teaspoon fish sauce
- 2 tablespoons fresh lime juice
- 1 tablespoon light brown sugar
- 1 bunch scallions, white part only, finely chopped
- 1 large garlic clove, minced or grated
- 1 small jalapeño, seeded and finely chopped
- 5 or 6 large tomatoes, sliced, or 1 pint cherry tomatoes, halved
- Fresh chopped basil and cilantro, for garnish (optional)

1. In a small bowl, combine the fish sauce, lime juice, brown sugar, scallions, garlic, and jalapeño. *Note: Depending on tastes, use more or less of the jalapeño.*
2. Arrange the tomatoes on a medium serving plate and spoon the dressing over them. Let stand for 10 minutes. Right before serving, sprinkle with basil and cilantro (if using).

There are many things to like about this salad. The color is bright green with splashes of red, a good contrast to the meat and potatoes. The taste is light and refreshing despite the preponderance of butter, and the salad holds well, ideal for advance preparation.

This dish is an adaptation of a recipe by Anjali Prasertong for The Kitchn *and makes more than enough salad for four people, so plan to have it on hand for another day or two. You will need a food processor with the slicing attachment to finely cut the Brussels sprouts.*

SHAVED BRUSSELS SPROUTS SALAD

SERVES 4 to 6 | EQUIPMENT: food processor

12 ounces Brussels sprouts

1 small crisp red apple

4 teaspoons fresh lemon juice (divided)

4 tablespoons unsalted butter

1 tablespoon white wine vinegar

½ teaspoon kosher salt

2 tablespoons grapeseed or other neutral oil

¼ cup coarsely chopped salted almonds

1. Trim off the ends of the Brussels sprouts. Using the slicing blade of the food processor, finely slice the sprouts. Empty the shredded sprouts into a large bowl.

2. Cut the apple into quarters and remove the core but leave on the skin for added color. Slice the apple with the food processor, remove the slices, and cut them by hand into ¼-inch pieces. Move them to a small bowl and sprinkle with 2 teaspoons of lemon juice.

3. Melt the butter in a small pan over medium heat. Swirl to distribute the butter and watch carefully. Cook until the butter starts to brown and smells nutty. It will be light brown with dark specs in it. To stop the cooking, pour immediately into a small heatproof measuring cup, brown bits and all. Let it cool a few minutes.

4. To make the dressing, in a small bowl whisk together the vinegar, the remaining 2 teaspoons of lemon juice, the salt, and oil. Once combined, slowly add the melted butter while whisking. Don't stop until you have a thick emulsified dressing. Taste and adjust the seasonings if needed.

5 Add the apples and nuts to the Brussels sprouts. Pour over the dressing and mix thoroughly. The salad can be made ahead of time and keeps well refrigerated for several hours or until the next day. If serving the next day, add the nuts just before serving.

6 Let the salad stand at room temperature for 30 minutes before serving.

Flan, though humble in ingredients, is an exceptional dessert when made correctly and caps off your informal Sunday dinner. Follow this recipe carefully and you'll have a flan that rivals the best of them. The low oven temperature and the small amount of cream cheese assure a silky texture with just the right amount of structure. Both of my sons, Eric and Neal, made it for their high school Spanish classes when their assignment required a regional food item, so it's not too difficult for Sunday dinner.

I originally received the recipe from my sister in the 1990s. I still remember her dictating the ingredients to me over the phone which I scribbled down in the back of Elena's Secrets of Mexican Cooking so I wouldn't lose it. I suppose this is my 'not so secret' Mexican dessert.

FLAN

SERVES 8 | EQUIPMENT: electric blender, large baking pan to hold a smaller 2-quart dish

¾ cup granulated sugar
4 large eggs
1 (14-ounce) can sweetened condensed milk
1¾ cups whole or 2% milk
2 ounces cream cheese, room temperature

1. Preheat the oven to 325°F

2. In a small heavy saucepan over medium-low heat, cook the sugar until it is melted and golden. Stir occasionally with a wooden spoon. This takes about 10 minutes. Watch carefully.

3. Once melted, quickly pour the caramel into an ungreased 2-quart baking dish, swirling the pan so that the caramel covers the bottom. (The liquid hardens on impact with the cool dish, but don't worry; after baking it will become a sweet sauce that flows over the creamy flan when turned onto the serving plate.) Set the dish aside.

4. Combine the eggs, condensed milk, whole milk, and cream cheese in a blender. Blend for 30 seconds, or until the ingredients are smooth and fully mixed. Pour the mixture into the caramel-filled baking dish.

5. Place the baking dish in a larger baking pan and pour boiling water into the larger pan to a depth of 1 inch. This water bath helps the flan cook slowly and evenly. Bake for 50 to 60 minutes, or until just set; the custard will jiggle in the middle when done and a knife inserted in the middle should come out clean. Low and slow is the secret to creamy flan; don't overcook. *Note: The circumference of your pan determines the cooking time. I use a 2-quart soufflé dish, which is 7¼ inches across, and it takes 55 minutes.*

6. When done, remove the dish from the oven and then from the water bath. The flan will continue to thicken as it cools. Cover and refrigerate overnight or as long as you can hold out, at least 4 hours.

7. To unmold, run a knife around the edges of the dish and invert onto a rimmed serving platter. The caramelized sugar makes a sauce and will spill out over and around the flan.

If you want to dress this up a bit, add a circle of raspberries around the perimeter and a dollop of whipped cream on each plate.

Spanakopita

Sun-Dried Tomato Dip on Pringles

Bacon and Pecan Pimento Cheese

Mango Guacamole Dip

Fresh Red Grapes

Flourless Orange and Almond Cookies

Chocolate-Truffle Cookies

Make Ahead
Up to 1 month before: Make the spanakopita and freeze.
Up to 3 days before: Make the dough for the almond cookies and refrigerate.
Day before: Make the pimento cheese, bake the almond cookies, make the tomato dip. Make the dough for the chocolate cookies.
Day of: Bake the chocolate cookies.
Up to 4 hours before: Make the guacamole dip.
Last hour: Pipe the tomato dip onto the chips, spread the pimento cheese on the crackers, bake the spanakopita.

WINE TASTING PARTY

A great wine tasting party, or more aptly named, "wine drinking party" is a fun and novel way to entertain a group, be they close friends or casual acquaintances. I learned the format from the Austin Rotary Club, but you can apply it to any group gathering. First decide on a wine-related theme, such as wine from a particular area or region, wines with great labels, or wines of a certain varietal. Ask each guest to bring a bottle and you supply the munchies. What's so appealing about this format is you'll never worry about running out of wine, and you'll actually end up with more wine than you could possibly drink. Also, you have the pleasure of planning a table full of wine-friendly appetizers.

I've hosted parties with themes of Argentinian wine (think empanadas and salsa dancing), French wines with Francophile hors d'oeuvres, and "summer sippin' wines" served with cool dips and other no-bake treats. I like to pair the appetizers with the theme, but it's not necessary. Good food is always appreciated, no matter the origin. Below is an assortment of appetizers that can be mixed and matched; all make good party food and go well with wine. Make sure there is some dark chocolate on the table, even if it is just M&M's; you'll be surprised by how quickly they go.

This recipe has been in my repertoire for over forty years. I suppose that's how long I have been collecting recipes. It was published in the children's Weekly Reader, *which I stumbled upon during my short career as a teacher at St. Thomas Aquinas school in Dallas. Inspiration lurks in the most unusual of places.*

What's great about this recipe is it can be prepared ahead of time and frozen. It's a little tedious to put together, so I suggest advanced preparation. I thought these little bite-size Greek pastries were so satisfying that I doubled the recipe and made them for my own wedding reception in 1997.

SPANAKOPITA

MAKES about 50 pastries | EQUIPMENT: pastry blender or fork, biscuit or other circular cutter, pastry brush

Pastry

- 1 (8-ounce) package cream cheese, room temperature
- 1 cup (2 sticks) unsalted butter, room temperature
- 2 cups sifted all-purpose flour, plus more for dusting
- ¼ teaspoon kosher salt

Filling

- 2 tablespoons extra-virgin olive oil
- 1 small onion, finely chopped
- 1 (10-ounce) package frozen chopped spinach, thawed and well drained
- ½ cup low-fat or full-fat cottage cheese
- ¼ pound feta cheese, crumbled
- 1 teaspoon kosher salt

Assembly

- ¼ teaspoon water
- 1 large egg, beaten
- ½ teaspoon sea salt

Pastry

1. In a medium bowl, use a fork to combine the cream cheese and butter. In a small bowl, mix the flour and the salt and add to the cream cheese mixture. Combine with a pastry blender or fork. Work the dough with your hands until it holds together. Divide the dough into two flat circles, wrap in plastic wrap, and chill overnight, or at least 4 hours.

2. Let the dough come to room temperature to soften. On a floured surface, roll the dough out to a ⅛-inch thickness. Using a biscuit cutter, cut it into 2½-inch circles.

Filling

1. Preheat the oven to 400°F and line a baking sheet with parchment paper (if baking right away).

2. Heat the oil until shimmering, then add the onion and sauté until softened, about 3 minutes. Remove from the heat and add the spinach, cottage cheese, feta cheese and salt. Blend well.

Assembly

1. Place ¾ teaspoon of the filling on each circle of dough. Fold the circle over and press the edges with a fork and prick the center. If the pastry is too warm to prick, place it in the refrigerator for about 15 minutes to harden. *Note: If freezing for later cooking, stack the pastries between wax paper to keep them from sticking together.*

2. Right before baking, mix together the water and egg in a small bowl. Using a pastry brush, brush the pastries with the egg mixture and sprinkle on the sea salt.

3. Transfer the pastries to the prepared baking sheet and bake for about 15 minutes, or until brown. Serve warm.

If frozen, let the pastries sit out at room temperature for 10 to 15 minutes so they can be easily separated.

Wild Turkey Kitchen

The assembled tomatoes and chips in this recipe look like little Stetson hats, bright and fanciful. They satisfy the all important raw vegetable option on your hors d'oeuvre table without resorting to the tired grocery store vegetable platter.

The tomato dip itself originally appeared in The Barefoot Contessa Cookbook *by Ina Garten. Ina's recipes are always spot on in ease of preparation and good taste. The presentation with the tomato on the potato chip is my invention. Don't be intimidated by the use of a pastry bag. Using disposable bags makes cleanup easy and no special skill is involved.*

SUN-DRIED TOMATO DIP ON PRINGLES

MAKES 2 cups | EQUIPMENT: food processor, pastry bag fitted with a star tip

¼ cup sun-dried tomatoes in oil, drained and chopped

1 (8-ounce package) cream cheese, room temperature (important or you will have lumps)

½ cup sour cream

½ cup good-quality mayonnaise, such as Hellmann's

10 dashes Tabasco chipotle sauce

1 teaspoon kosher salt

¾ teaspoon ground black pepper

2 scallions, white and green parts, thinly sliced

1 pint cherry tomatoes, halved

1 (5.2-ounce) can Pringles

1. Place the sun-dried tomatoes, cream cheese, sour cream, mayonnaise, Tabasco sauce, salt, and pepper in a food processor fitted with a metal blade. Pulse the mixture to combine. Add the scallions and pulse twice more.

2. Transfer the dip to a pastry bag fitted with an open star tip that is large enough for the sun-dried tomatoes to pass through. Pipe a dollop of dip onto the middle of each chip, add a half tomato on top of the dip, and press gently.

3. Serve within the hour.

You can make the dip ahead of time, but let it come to room temperature before piping. I've made these 30 minutes before the party starts and they have been fine sitting out for the evening, but the chips will get soggy sitting out any longer.

Whether you view pimento cheese as humble and old-fashioned or as trendy and gourmet, it's a spread worthy of your party. Known by some as "southern caviar," it began inauspiciously in the 1900s in New York where mass-produced cream cheese and imported Spanish pimiento peppers were plentiful. Owing to its popularity, an enterprising Georgian farmer began growing pimentos to reduce the high cost of the imported peppers. Later when pimento canning was introduced in East Tennessee, the southern region of the US embraced the spread as a southern speciality and improved on the flavor with the substitution of cheddar cheese.

Growing up in Texas, pimento cheese sandwiches were on frequent rotation in my lunch box. The ingredients were simple: grated cheddar cheese, pimentos, and Hellmann's mayonnaise. As with so many food trends, pimento cheese is back in vogue and add-ins abound. This recipe introduces complexity with the addition of bacon, pecans, and spices. I like to serve it already spread on a good sturdy cracker or crostini so guests can grab a bite one handed. The bacon can be rather salty, so add salt carefully and taste after each addition. This makes a lot and can easily be halved.

The recipe was adapted from The Splendid Table, *who reprinted it from* The Bourbon Country Cookbook *by David Danielson and Tim Laird.*

BACON AND PECAN PIMENTO CHEESE

MAKES 3 cups | EQUIPMENT: stand mixer or food processor

- 24 ounces sharp yellow cheddar cheese, grated (about 6 cups)
- 1 cup good-quality mayonnaise, such as Hellmann's
- 1 (4-ounce) jar diced pimentos, drained
- ¼ cup pecan pieces, toasted (see note on page 41)
- ½ cup diced cooked bacon (about 8 strips)
- ½ tablespoon Dijon mustard
- Pinch cayenne pepper
- Pinch celery salt
- Kosher salt and ground black pepper, to taste
- Crackers, for serving

1. In the bowl of a stand mixer with a paddle attachment, combine the cheddar cheese, mayonnaise, pimentos, pecans, bacon, mustard, cayenne pepper, and celery salt. Beat on medium speed for 2 minutes, or until well combined. A food processor can be used in place of the mixer.

2. Taste and add salt and pepper if needed. Store in an airtight container and refrigerate for up to 1 week.

3. Let stand at room temperature for 30 minutes before spreading on crackers to serve.

To toast pecans, preheat the oven to 325°F. Place the pecans on a rimmed baking sheet and bake for 5 to 7 minutes, until the nuts begin to brown and become fragrant; watch closely.

Guacamole dip is the bread and butter of casual get-togethers in Texas. Costco makes an incredibly good one, so no matter the season, you're sure to find this dip at the best of parties. Wanting to distinguish my guacamole from the crowd, I found an interesting twist on the traditional version from a recipe originally published in Gourmet *magazine in November 2008 by Lillian Chou.*

By adding mango to the mix, the dip takes on a tropical air. The fruit is a nice contrast to the silky flesh of the avocado, while the added sweetness of it balances the acidity of the lemons.

MANGO GUACAMOLE DIP

MAKES 4 cups

4 ripe avocados
1 cup finely chopped sweet onion
1 teaspoon serrano chile, finely chopped (include seeds only if you want it really hot)
¼ cup fresh lemon juice
1¼ teaspoons kosher salt
1 cup diced peeled mango (about 1 large mango)
½ cup chopped fresh cilantro
Corn chips, for serving

1. Halve, pit, and peel the avocados.
2. Coarsely mash them in a medium bowl. Stir in the onion, chile, lemon juice, and salt.
3. Fold in the mango and cilantro. Taste and add more salt and lemon juice if needed. Don't be shy with the lemon juice; it is the distinguishing feature of a flavorful guacamole.
4. Serve with any type of corn chip.

Guacamole can be made 4 hours ahead of time and chilled. When chilling, cover the surface so it is airtight with plastic wrap. Bring to room temperature and stir before serving.

This is a great cookie; not only is it very flavorful and a little unusual but it also satisfies the gluten-free crowd. An added benefit to these cookies is the make-ahead options. The logs of dough can be prepared up to three days before baking, or they can be baked ahead of time and stored in an airtight container at room temperature for up to three days.

The recipe was inspired by a 2016 recipe by Louisa Shafia in Epicurious. *To make the original recipe, replace the vanilla and orange extract with 1½ teaspoons ground cardamon and replace the almonds with salted pistachios. Though easy to prepare, they require 2½ hours of refrigeration before baking, so plan accordingly.*

FLOURLESS ORANGE AND ALMOND COOKIES

MAKES 30 cookies | EQUIPMENT: electric mixer, microwave

- 1 cup granulated sugar
- ⅓ cup virgin coconut oil, room temperature
- 1 large egg
- 2 tablespoons grated orange zest (about 3 small oranges)
- 1 teaspoon vanilla extract
- ¼ teaspoon orange extract

- 2 cups almond flour
- ¼ cup potato starch
- ¼ teaspoon kosher salt
- ½ cup finely chopped roasted salted almonds
- 3 ounces dark chocolate, for drizzling (optional)

1. In a large bowl, cream the sugar and coconut oil with an electric mixer on medium speed until the mixture resembles the texture of wet sand, about 3 minutes.
2. Add the egg, orange zest, vanilla, and orange extract. Beat until just combined. Set aside.
3. In a medium bowl, whisk together the almond flour, potato starch, and salt.
4. Fold the flour mixture into the sugar mixture. Cover with plastic wrap and chill for 1 hour.
5. Spread the almonds in a single layer on a sheet of wax paper. Set aside. Divide the chilled dough into 2 balls, then roll each ball into a 1½-inch-diameter log. Roll the logs in the chopped almonds to lightly coat; reserve any remaining almonds for decorating.

6. Wrap the logs in plastic wrap and chill again, this time for 1½ hours or up to 3 days.

7. Preheat the oven to 350°F and position the oven racks in the upper and lower thirds of the oven.

8. Line two baking sheets with parchment paper.

9. Slice the dough into ¼-inch rounds and arrange on the prepared baking sheets 1 inch apart. Sprinkle with the reserved almonds and press them lightly to adhere. The additional almonds are optional, as you may want to drizzle some with melted chocolate after they bake and leave others with almonds only.

10. Bake the cookies, rotating the sheets from front to back and top to bottom halfway through, until the undersides are golden, 8 to 12 minutes. The tops will be a little soft. Transfer to wire racks for cooling.

11. If a third batch is needed, let the baking sheet cool completely before lining with parchment and baking.

12. Break the chocolate (if using) into pieces and place in a microwave-safe bowl. Melt it in 10 second bursts in the microwave, stirring the chocolate between bursts, until the chocolate is smooth.

13. Drizzle the cooled cookies with the chocolate and let set before serving.

All wine tastings should feature a chocolate option. These dark chocolate cookies are soft and chock full of chocolate, better than candy. They are best served warm, but given all the last minute preparations for a party, it's fine to serve them at room temperature. This recipe was adapted from Joy Wilson's recipe published in Joy the Baker Homemade Decadence, *which was reprinted in 2014 on* Epicurious.

CHOCOLATE-TRUFFLE COOKIES

MAKES about 30 cookies

1 cup all-purpose flour
1 cup granulated sugar
½ cup unsweetened Dutch-process cocoa powder
1 teaspoon baking powder
½ teaspoon kosher salt
2 teaspoons instant espresso powder
2 large eggs
2 tablespoons vanilla extract
4 tablespoons unsalted butter, cut into pieces, room temperature
⅔ cup chopped dark chocolate (about 6 ounces)
½ cup chopped pecans (optional)
1 cup powdered sugar

1. In a medium bowl, whisk together the flour, granulated sugar, cocoa powder, baking powder, salt, and espresso powder. Set aside.

2. In a separate small bowl, whisk together the eggs and vanilla. Set aside.

3. With clean hands, rub the butter into the flour and sugar mixture until the mixture resembles bread crumbs. Stir in the chocolate and pecans (if using).

4. Add the egg mixture to the chocolate mixture, stirring with a fork until slightly moistened and gooey. Form the dough into a ball and wrap in plastic wrap; refrigerate for 60 minutes or up to 1 day.

5. Preheat the oven to 375°F. Line two baking sheets with parchment paper. Place the powdered sugar in a wide narrow shallow bowl.

6. Shape the dough into tablespoon-size balls. Roll each in powdered sugar to coat, then place them on the prepared baking sheets 2-inches apart. Bake until just set but still slightly undercooked, about 10 minutes. *Note: This is critical; it's the difference between a soft or crispy cookie.*

7. Cool for 5 minutes on the baking sheets, then move to a wire rack to cool completely.

Cheese Böreks

Chicken Paprikas

Vegetable Toss

Provincial Cherry Tomato Gratin

Mexican Chocolate Pepita Cake
with Candied Ancho Chiles
or
Awesome Coconut Cake

Make Ahead
Up to 1 month before: Bake the layers for the coconut cake and freeze or prepare the chocolate cake and freeze.
Up to 2 weeks before: Make the Cheese Böreks and freeze.
Up to 2 days before: Make the raspberry sauce for the chocolate cake.
Day before: Make the Chicken Paprikas, toast the coconut for the coconut cake, defrost the frozen cake in the refrigerator.
Morning of: String the sugar snap peas for the Vegetable Toss, assemble the tomato gratin, make the frosting or the ganache and ice either cake.
Last hour: Assemble the ingredients for the Vegetable Toss, bake the Cheese Böreks, boil the noodles or rice, bake the tomato gratin, heat the Chicken Paprikas.

BIRTHDAY CELEBRATION

My favorite birthday gift for the over twenty-one crowd is a birthday cake or better yet, a birthday dinner. Celebrating with a round cake and candles dates back to a thirteenth-century German tradition, Kinderfeste, where children's birthdays were a day-long affair ending in dinner, cake, and presents. I embrace this tradition; few can resist sharing a birthday cake, much less a dinner in their honor.

One of my more notable birthday celebration meals was the "Salute to Julia Child" dinner for my brother-in-law, where every recipe was one of Julia's and every pan in my kitchen received a strenuous workout. Another memorable occasion was the "Beer Pairing" birthday meal for my beer aficionado husband. The party started off with a light wheat ale served with the appetizers, progressed through multiple courses of delight, and ended with a chocolate stout for dessert.

The meal presented here is special because it includes gluten-free options, which like it or not, is a necessity in many families. I've included two dessert choices, and one can be prepared gluten-free.

Cheese Böreks, Turkish pastries with a savory filling, are a guaranteed crowd-pleasing appetizer. I discovered them back in the eighties in a fundraising cookbook for the New Stage Theater in Jackson, Mississippi, called Standing Room Only: A Cookbook for Entertaining. *This recipe alone saved the book from a trip to the thrift store.*

The original recipe had few instructions on exactly how the böreks should look, so over the years, I've played with the size and shape of them as well as the toppings. The size described below is perfect for a first course. Serve them plated with a fork and napkin to handle the oozing cheese and buttery goodness.

This recipe cannot be made gluten-free, so I suggest substituting the Italian Skewers (see page 145) for a gluten-free appetizer.

CHEESE BÖREKS

SERVES 12 as an appetizer | EQUIPMENT: pastry brush

2 large eggs
½ pound mozzarella cheese, grated
½ pound feta cheese, crumbled
1 pint low- or full-fat cottage cheese
1 tablespoon chopped parsley
12 sheets phyllo pastry, defrosted if frozen

½ cup (1 stick) unsalted butter, melted and cooled
1 large egg yolk
2 teaspoons water
Sesame seeds or poppy seeds, for topping

1. Preheat the oven to 375°F. Line two baking sheets with parchment paper.
2. In a small bowl, lightly beat the eggs then mix in the mozzarella, feta, and cottage cheeses. Stir in the parsley.
3. Lightly dampen a kitchen towel and have it available as you work with the pastry.
4. Carefully unroll one piece of phyllo and brush it lightly with butter, being careful not to tear it. Cover the remainder of the pastry with its plastic packaging, followed by a kitchen towel, being careful not to let the damp towel come in direct contact with the stack as it's very difficult to separate the individual sheets if they are wet.

5. Put a heaping tablespoon of filling in the middle of the top third of the pastry, fold down the top to cover the filling, then fold in the sides and roll up. Your börek should be around 4 to 5 inches long. Phyllo sheets come in different sizes, so you may need to cut your sheets to get the size you want. They are typically about 9-by-14 inches. Stop here if freezing.

6. Whisk together the egg yolk and water until smooth. Brush a very light layer of egg wash over the top of each börek. Don't let the egg wash puddle or pool on the surface; a light layer works best. Sprinkle with sesame seeds.

7. Bake on the prepared baking sheets for 20 to 25 minutes, until golden. It's normal for the filling to ooze out the side. Serve warm for best flavor.

For make-ahead preparation, store the filled pastry in a freezer for up to two weeks. To store, place the unbaked pastries in an airtight container or plastic bag in single layers, separating each layer with a piece of parchment or wax paper. When ready to bake, take out of the freezer (no need to defrost) and proceed with the recipe. Frozen pastries will take a few minutes longer to bake, so watch carefully.

I owe my discovery of this dish to my sister's trip to Hungary. On her return, she presented me with a small foil packet of sweet paprika. To celebrate this special gift, I prepared a Hungarian-inspired meal for her. This was before the proliferation of internet recipes, so I turned to my reliable recipe source, Joy of Cooking. Over the years I've tinkered with the ingredients and method and have served it at many dinner parties. The original recipe calls for bone-in chicken pieces, but I've opted for skinless chicken breasts with a cooking method espoused by America's Test Kitchen.

The paprika gives the dish a beautiful rich reddish pink color, evoking spiciness. On the contrary, the flavor is quite mild, so it's important to use true fresh Hungarian sweet paprika. Buying from reputable online sources, such as The Spice House, make all the difference in finding the right ingredient for this subtly spiced dish. Remember to store any leftover spice in the freezer, as the paprika loses its flavor very quickly. If you like it hot, increase the cayenne by ¼ teaspoon.

This dish is traditionally served with noodles, but rice works just as well. Time improves the flavor, so I suggest making it a day ahead. Substitute gluten-free flour for the standard flour for the gluten intolerant.

CHICKEN PAPRIKAS

SERVES 6

- 1½ pounds boneless, skinless chicken breasts
- 1 tablespoon extra-virgin olive oil
- 3 cups chicken broth
- 1 tablespoon unsalted butter
- 3 cups thinly sliced onions (about 2 medium onions)
- ¼ cup Hungarian sweet paprika
- 2 tablespoons all-purpose flour
- ¼ teaspoon cayenne pepper
- 2 tablespoons minced garlic
- 1 large bay leaf
- ½ teaspoon kosher salt, plus more for seasoning chicken
- ½ teaspoon ground black pepper, plus more for seasoning chicken
- 1 to 1½ cups sour cream
- 1 medium lemon, cut into wedges, for squeezing
- 1 tablespoon chopped parsley
- Noodles or rice, for serving

1. Ensure chicken breasts are a uniform ½-inch thickness by pounding them between two sheets of wax paper or plastic wrap. This prevents uneven cooking. Season with salt and pepper.

2. In a 12-inch skillet over medium-high heat, heat the oil until shimmering. Add the chicken in a single layer and cook on one side until lightly brown, about 3 minutes. Lower the heat to medium low, flip the chicken, add the chicken broth, cover, and simmer for 5 to 6 minutes, or until the internal temperature registers 160°F on a digital thermometer. Watch carefully so the chicken does not overcook.

3. Move the chicken to a cutting board and shred into bite-size pieces. Cover and set aside. Strain the chicken broth to remove any white foam; set it aside for later use.

4. Wipe the skillet clean and reduce the heat to medium, heat the butter until shimmering, then add the onions. Cook the onions, stirring often, until they are just beginning to color, about 10 minutes.

5. Sprinkle the paprika, flour, and cayenne pepper over the onions and cook while stirring for 1 minute. Add 2 cups of the reserved chicken broth, the garlic, bay leaf, ½ teaspoon of salt, and ½ teaspoon of pepper.

6. Bring to a boil while stirring constantly. Reduce the heat to low, cover the skillet, and simmer gently for 30 minutes, stirring occasionally.

7. Discard the bay leaf and boil the sauce over high heat until very thick, almost pasty. This will not take long. Remove the pan from the heat and add the sour cream. Return the sauce to high heat and boil until thickened. Season to taste with salt and pepper.

8. Add the shredded chicken to the sauce and warm over medium heat, then squeeze a few drops of fresh lemon juice over the dish.

9. Place the chicken on a serving plate, garnish with the parsley, and serve with noodles or rice.

The chicken and sauce can be made the day before. Cover and refrigerate. To serve, reheat on the stove top with the cover on.

One of my favorite quick-to-prepare vegetable recipes is based on Lynne Rossetto Kasper's Three-Pea Toss found in her book How to Eat Supper. *Don't worry about precise measuring or these exact ingredients. Any stir-fried vegetable, like diced zucchini or sliced mushroom, can be substituted for the peas. Assembly is quick, and the barely cooked vegetables compliment a menu featuring spicy or creamy dishes.*

VEGETABLE TOSS

SERVES 4 to 6

1 cup frozen peas
1 heaping cup sugar snap peas
2 tablespoons extra-virgin olive oil
1 medium red onion, diced
Generous pinch granulated sugar

Kosher salt and ground black pepper
1 medium red bell pepper, diced
2 tablespoons chopped fresh mint leaves
½ cup coarsely chopped salted almonds

1. Set the peas out to partially thaw while preparing the rest of the dish.
2. If needed, string the sugar snap peas. To string the peas, with a small blunt knife, grasp the stem between your thumb and the blade and pull down the length of the pea pod.
3. Heat the oil in a large sauté pan over high heat until shimmering. Add the onion and sugar. Season to taste with salt and pepper. Stir over high heat for 1 minute.
4. Add the bell pepper and toss for 1 minute.
5. Stir in the snap peas and cook for 30 more seconds.
6. Add the defrosted peas and stir-fry for another 30 seconds, or until they are warmed.
7. Turn the vegetables onto a serving plate and toss with the mint and almonds. Serve immediately.

For years Julia Child's Stuffed Tomatoes Provençal was my go-to party side dish, but that was before I stumbled on Ina Garten's ingenious combination of cherry tomatoes and coarse bread crumbs. Unlike dismal-tasting off-season tomatoes, cherry tomatoes are flavorful no matter the season, and even better, no peeling or seeding is required.

This gratin looks beautiful alongside the brilliant greens of the Vegetable Toss and the rich pink of the Chicken Paprikas. For a gluten-free option, substitute gluten-free bread crumbs for the country bread.

PROVINCIAL CHERRY TOMATO GRATIN

SERVES 6 to 8 | EQUIPMENT: food processor

3 pints cherry or grape tomatoes, halved
1½ tablespoons extra-virgin olive oil, plus ¼ cup
1 teaspoon dried thyme
1½ teaspoons kosher salt (divided)
1 teaspoon ground black pepper (divided)
3 large garlic cloves
⅓ cup chopped parsley
2 cups coarse bread cubes from country bread, crusts removed

1. Preheat the oven to 400°F.
2. In a medium bowl, toss together the tomatoes, 1½ tablespoons oil, the thyme, 1 teaspoon of salt, and ½ teaspoon of pepper.
3. Spread the tomato mixture evenly in a 9-by-13-inch pan, making sure the pan is now coated with oil.
4. In a food processor fitted with a steel blade, pulse the garlic and the remaining ½ teaspoon of salt and ½ teaspoon of pepper. Process until the garlic is finely chopped, then add the parsley and bread cubes. Pulse until the bread is in crumbs. Add the remaining ¼ cup of oil and pulse a few more times to blend.
5. Sprinkle the crumb mixture evenly over the tomatoes. *Note: Can be made ahead to this point by covering and refrigerating until time to bake.*
6. Bake the gratin until the crumbs are golden and the tomato juices are bubbling, 40 to 45 minutes. Serve hot or warm.

Rick Bayless, the award-winning chef who specializes in traditional Mexican cuisine, originally authored this recipe. I adapted it for an entry in a cooking competition by tinkering with the ingredients and enhancing the presentation with two sauces and a topping of chocolate ganache. I won the competition, and you'll win the praise of your birthday guests.

This cake is versatile, and even at its most basic, is delicious. For a much simpler cake, leave out the candied ancho chiles completely and skip the sauces. Replace the ganache with a sprinkle of cocoa. Since toasted pepitas arc the main binder in the recipe, the cake lends itself well to gluten-free flour. Pepitas are often sold as "shelled pumpkin seeds", so regardless of the labeling, they are interchangeable in this recipe.

The sauces take time, so I suggest starting this cake a day before the party or bake the cake weeks ahead and freeze. I've tried it with both Mexican bittersweet chocolate and grocery store brand chocolate bars that are at least 60% chocolate and find little difference in flavor. Both produce an excellent cake.

MEXICAN CHOCOLATE PEPITA CAKE WITH CANDIED ANCHO CHILES

SERVES 8 | EQUIPMENT: kitchen shears, 9-inch round cake pan, food processor

- 8 tablespoons (1 stick) unsalted butter, cut into ½-inch pieces, room temperature, plus 2 tablespoons for greasing pan
- 2 to 3 large ancho chili pods, stemmed (about 2 ounces)
- ¾ cup water
- 1¾ cups granulated sugar, plus 2 tablespoons
- 1¾ cups toasted salted pepitas (divided)
- 3 large eggs, room temperature
- 1 tablespoon tequila
- ⅓ cup all-purpose flour or gluten-free flour
- ¼ teaspoon baking powder
- Pinch cayenne or chipotle chile powder
- ¼ teaspoon ancho chile powder (optional)
- ½ cup chopped (pea-size) bittersweet chocolate bar or Mexican chocolate (about 3 ounces)
- Chocolate Ganache (recipe follows)
- Raspberry Sauce (recipe follows)
- Vanilla Custard Sauce (recipe follows)

1. Preheat the oven to 350°F. Line a plate with parchment paper.

2. Grease the bottom and sides of a 9-inch cake pan with 1 tablespoon of butter. Line the bottom of the pan with a circle of parchment paper and slather the parchment with the other tablespoon of butter.

3. Prepare the ancho chiles by first removing the tiny seeds. The easiest way to do this is with kitchen shears while the chiles are completely dry. Slit open each chile with the shears and scrape out the seeds. Next use the shears to cut the chiles into strips, then bunch the strips together and cut into ¼-inch squares.

4. In a small saucepan over medium heat, bring the water and ¾ cup of sugar to a simmer while stirring to dissolve the sugar. Add the chiles and simmer for 5 minutes. Place a wire strainer over a bowl and toss in the wet chiles. Give the strainer a few shakes and then dump the candied chiles onto the prepared plate to dry. The chile simple syrup can be saved and used for adding a little punch to your cocktails.

5. Prepare the bottom of the pan by sprinkling ½ cup of the pepitas over the buttered parchment, then evenly sprinkling 2 tablespoons of the sugar over the pumpkin seeds. Set aside.

6. In the bowl of the a food processor fitted with the metal blade, add the remaining 1¼ cups of pepitas and the remaining 1 cup of sugar. Pulse until the seeds are pulverized and resemble coarse sand.

7. Add the eggs, the remaining stick of butter, and tequila. Pulse until incorporated.

8. Add the flour, baking powder, cayenne chile powder, and ancho chile powder (if using). Pulse just until combined and you have a smooth batter.

9. Add the chocolate and the candied chiles to the batter. Pulse two or three times until mixed.

10. Scrape the batter into the prepared pan and place in the lower third of the preheated oven. Bake for 35 to 40 minutes, until a toothpick inserted in the middle comes out clean. You may have to cover the pan with aluminum foil during the last 5 minutes to prevent a dark crust from forming.

11. Cool the cake on a wire rack for 10 minutes.

12. Loosen the sides of the cake by scraping the sides of the pan with a knife. Upend the pan on to a flat serving plate and carefully remove the parchment paper. The cake will have a crunchy layer on top from the candied pepitas. The top looks lighter than the bottom and the sides of the cake.

Recipe continued on next page

13 When the cake is completely cool, squeeze the chocolate ganache over the cake in vertical lines, then in horizontal lines to form a free-form checkered pattern. To serve, on each individual plate, squeeze four lines of raspberry sauce on the plate. Between each line of raspberry sauce, squeeze a thin line of vanilla custard sauce. Drag a toothpick or knife through both sauces to create a swivel effect.

Chocolate Ganache

Chocolate ganache is a versatile, never fail icing, glaze or filling. Made with bittersweet chocolate, it's not overly sweet, and leftovers can be warmed and drizzled over ice cream.

MAKES about 1 cup | EQUIPMENT: plastic squeeze bottle, funnel

- ½ cup heavy cream
- 8 ounces bittersweet chocolate, chopped into small pieces
- 1 teaspoon vanilla extract
- 1 tablespoon corn syrup

1. Heat the cream in a small saucepan over medium-low heat until just simmering. Remove from the heat.
2. Add the chocolate and stir until melted.
3. Add the vanilla and corn syrup. Stir to combine.
4. Using a funnel, pour the ganache into a plastic squeeze bottle and cool at room temperature before using.

Refrigerate leftovers for up to a month. To use again, warm for 5 to 10 seconds in the microwave or run the bottle under warm water.

Raspberry Sauce

This simple raspberry sauce adds color to the plate and a little tartness for contrast with the sugary cake.

MAKES 1¼ cups | EQUIPMENT: fine mesh strainer, funnel, electric blender, plastic squeeze bottle

12 ounces frozen raspberries
3 tablespoons granulated sugar
1 teaspoon fresh lemon juice

1 teaspoon kirsch or other berry or orange flavored liqueur (optional)

1. In a medium saucepan over low heat, combine the raspberries and sugar. Bring to a boil, stirring occasionally.
2. Cook the mixture for about 5 minutes, allowing it to boil very slowly. Stop cooking when the sauce is slightly thickened.
3. Cool the mixture, then puree in a blender. Stir and press the berries through a fine mesh strainer to remove the seeds. This is tedious but makes a beautiful smooth sauce. If you don't mind the seeds, then skip the straining.
4. Stir in the lemon juice and the liqueur (if using).
5. Using a funnel, pour the berry sauce into a plastic squeeze bottle and cool completely before using.

Refrigerate leftovers for up to a week.

Vanilla Custard Sauce

This sauce is almost a crème anglaise, but this light version has fewer eggs, making it more suitable for a rich cake. Most vanilla sauce recipes call for vanilla beans, but weighing the cost over the finished product, I think substituting vanilla extract is fine.

MAKES 2 cups | EQUIPMENT: digital thermometer, fine mesh strainer, funnel, plastic squeeze bottle

2 large eggs
½ cup granulated sugar

1 cup heavy cream
1 cup whole milk
1 teaspoon vanilla extract

1. In a heatproof bowl, whisk together the eggs and sugar and set aside.
2. In a 2- to 3-quart heavy saucepan over medium-low heat, heat the cream and milk until just beginning to simmer. Watch for tiny bubbles around the perimeter of the pan, then remove from the heat.
3. Slowly add half of the warm mixture, in a slow stream, to the eggs and sugar, whisking constantly.
4. Transfer the sugar mixture to the saucepan and cook over medium-low heat, stirring constantly with a wooden spoon. Continue to cook until the mixture has thickened and the custard registers 175°F on a digital thermometer, 5 to 10 minutes. Do not let the mixture boil.
5. Off the heat, add in the vanilla, then pour the custard through a fine mesh strainer, discarding any solids. Place the bowl in a larger bowl containing ice and water. Stir the custard as it cools.
6. Using a funnel, pour the custard into a plastic squeeze bottle and refrigerate for at least 1 hour before using.

Refrigerate leftovers for up to two days.

This is an all-time great cake. I've made it for birthdays, Easter, and whenever in need of a beautiful tender cake. It's suitable for cupcakes, or divide the recipe in half for a single layer cake when the only occasion is your craving for a sweet ending to a weeknight meal.

This cake originally appeared in a Bon Appétit *article in 1999. A reader requested the recipe from the Shubox Cafe in Cedar Grove, New Jersey, and while the cafe is long gone, the cake aptly named Awesome Coconut Cake, lives on.*

AWESOME COCONUT CAKE

SERVES 8 to 12 | EQUIPMENT: 2 (9-inch) round cake pans, electric mixer

- 2¾ cups all-purpose flour, plus more for the pans
- 1 teaspoon baking powder
- ½ teaspoon baking soda
- ½ teaspoon kosher salt
- 1¾ cups granulated sugar
- 1 cup (2 sticks) unsalted butter, room temperature, plus more for greasing
- 1 cup canned sweetened coconut cream
- 4 large eggs, separated, room temperature
- 1 teaspoon vanilla extract
- 1 cup buttermilk
- Pinch kosher salt
- Coconut Cream Cheese Frosting (recipe follows)
- 4 cups sweetened shredded coconut, toasted (see tip on page 63)

1. Preheat the oven to 350°F. Butter and flour two (9-inch) cake pans.
2. Sift the flour, baking powder, baking soda, and salt into a medium bowl, then whisk to blend.
3. In the large bowl of a stand mixer fitted with the paddle attachment, or in a large bowl if using a hand-held mixer, beat the sugar, butter, and sweetened coconut cream until fluffy. Beat in the egg yolks, one at a time, and then the vanilla.
4. On low speed, beat in the flour mixture and the buttermilk, alternating between the two, starting and ending with the flour. Beat until just blended.
5. In another large bowl using clean dry beaters, beat the egg whites with a pinch of salt until stiff but not dry. Carefully fold the beaten egg whites into the batter.

6. Divide the cake batter between the prepared pans. Bake the cakes until a tester inserted into the center comes out clean, about 45 minutes.

7. Cool the cakes in their pans on a wire rack for 10 minutes. When cool, run a small sharp knife around the sides of the pan to loosen the cakes. Turn the cakes out onto the rack and cool completely while you prepare the toasted coconut.

8. Place a cake layer on a cake plate and spread 1 cup of the frosting over the cake layer. Sprinkle 1 cup of the shredded coconut over the top. Top with the second cake layer. Spread the remaining frosting over the top and sides of the cake. Sprinkle the remaining 3 cups of coconut over the cake, using gentle pressure to adhere the coconut to the sides.

This cake can be prepared up to one day ahead. Cover with plastic wrap and refrigerate. Let it stand at room temperature 2 hours before serving. The cake layers can also be made up to a month ahead of time, wrapped tightly and frozen.

To toast the coconut, spread the shredded coconut on a parchment-lined rimmed baking sheet in a thin layer. Toast in a 325°F degree oven for 5 to 7 minutes. Stir after a few minutes to ensure even browning. Watch carefully, as coconut burns easily. Can be prepared a day ahead and stored in an airtight freezer bag.

Coconut Cream Cheese Frosting

This is a traditional cream cheese frosting with an added boost of flavor from the coconut cream.

MAKES enough to fill and frost 2 (9-inch) layers | EQUIPMENT: electric mixer

2 (8-ounce) packages cream cheese, room temperature
½ cup (1 stick) unsalted butter, room temperature
2 cups powdered sugar, sifted
½ cup canned sweetened coconut cream
1 teaspoon vanilla extract

1. In the bowl of a stand mixer fitted with the paddle attachment, or in a large bowl if using a hand-held mixer, cream together the cream cheese and butter until fluffy, 3 to 5 minutes.

2. Add the sugar, sweetened coconut cream, and vanilla and beat until well blended.

Candied Bacon Bites

Assorted Cheese and Crackers

Chicken Vegetable Cobbler

Waldorf Salad

Sweet and Spicy Candied Pecans

Fresh Tomato and Cucumber Salad

Lemon Cake

Dark Chocolate Pudding with Toasted Coconut

Make Ahead

Up to 3 days before: Make the candied pecans.
Up to 2 days before: Make the pudding, toast the coconut.
Day before: Prepare the cobbler (do not bake), bake the cake.
Morning of: Cook the candied bacon, mix the spread for the bacon bites, make the cobbler crust, make the tomato and cucumber mixture, mix the dressing.
Afternoon of: Prepare the Waldorf Salad, glaze the cake or sprinkle with powdered sugar. Whip the cream for the pudding.
Last hour: Assemble the bacon bites, arrange the cheese and crackers, bake the cobbler, finish the Fresh Tomato and Cucumber Salad.

BUNCO PARTY OR DINNER FOR TWELVE

I'm not a Bunco player, but several of my close friends are avid "Bunco Babes"; their term not mine. Over the years, I've witnessed white knuckles and furrowed brows as they anticipate their turn at hosting. I understand the concern. Preparing a meal for twelve women, usually on a week night, is daunting for even experienced cooks.

Included is a light menu serving twelve, along with make-ahead suggestions to ease the stress. Even at fairly formal sit-down meals, I've observed most serve themselves modest portions but save room for dessert, and the wine always flows. These recipes are certainly not limited to a Bunco party and are great for any gathering, especially when serving those with lighter appetites.

Serve these sweet and savory appetizers along with a cheese and cracker platter while the group gathers. They were inspired by a candied bacon bourbon cocktail, but they go well with wine or beer.

CANDIED BACON BITES

MAKES about 36 bites | EQUIPMENT: pastry brush, wire rack, food processor

1 (12-ounce) package bacon
4 tablespoons maple syrup
1/3 cup packed light or dark brown sugar
Pinch cayenne pepper (optional)
1 (8-ounce) package cream cheese, room temperature
1/2 cup grated Pecorino Romano
2 tablespoons finely chopped fresh dill
Wafer thin crackers or a loaf of ciabatta bread, sliced and toasted with extra-virgin olive oil and cut into bite-size pieces.

1. Preheat the oven to 325°F. Line two rimmed baking sheets with aluminum foil and top with a wire rack.

2. Lay out the bacon on the wire rack. You'll only fit half of the package on each sheet so repeat the process if you only have one sheet.

3. Brush both sides of the bacon with the maple syrup.

4. Combine the brown sugar and cayenne (if using) and sprinkle the mixture evenly over the bacon, on the top side only.

5. Bake for 20 minutes, but watch the bacon carefully. Continue to check every 3 to 5 minutes until the bacon is crispy on the ends but not burned. This could take an additional 5 to 10 minutes, depending on your oven and the thickness of the bacon.

6. When cooked, use tongs to place the bacon onto parchment paper for cooling.

7. While the bacon is cooking, prepare the spread by combining in a food processor the cream cheese, grated cheese, and dill.

8. Top the crackers with the cream cheese spread, then with the candied bacon pieces, and serve at room temperature.

To prepare ciabatta bread, use a pastry brush to lightly spread olive oil on one side and toast in a 375°F oven for 3 minutes on each side.

Throughout the years, I've made many chicken pot pies, but this adaptation of a Williams Sonoma recipe tops the list. In addition to being chock-full of flavorful vegetables, the make-ahead preparation ensures your sanity. The dish keeps well for a day in the refrigerator, sans crust, or complete it entirely and freeze for up to a month.

A cobbler style crust crowns this pie, but your favorite pie crust or even frozen puff pastry substitute nicely. To save a little time, my poultry preference is a grocery store roasted chicken with its tender meat and easy deboning. The flavorful carcass freezes well for later use in chicken stock. Optionally poach your own chicken, or it's a perfect dish for leftover turkey. Both frozen and fresh vegetables contribute texture and flavor, but the mushrooms prepared à la Julia Child set this dish apart from others.

I've served this to twelve women, along with the rest of this menu, and still had a little cobbler left over.

CHICKEN VEGETABLE COBBLER

SERVES 8 to 12 | EQUIPMENT: pastry blender, pastry brush

Filling

- 2½ cups frozen pearl onions
- 1 cup frozen petite English peas
- 1 cup frozen corn kernels
- 10 tablespoons (1¼ sticks) unsalted butter (divided)
- 3 medium carrots, peeled and cut into ¼-inch cubes
- 1 leek, white and light green parts only, finely chopped
- 1 tablespoon extra-virgin olive oil (divided)
- 1 pound fresh mushrooms, coarsely chopped
- 4 cups diced cooked chicken
- 7 tablespoons all-purpose flour
- 2 cups chicken broth
- 1 cup half-and-half
- 1 teaspoon kosher salt
- ½ teaspoon ground black pepper
- 2 tablespoons finely chopped parsley
- 2 tablespoons finely chopped fresh dill

Recipe continued on next page

Cobbler Dough

1¾ cups all-purpose flour, plus more for dusting

1 tablespoon baking powder

¼ teaspoon kosher salt

6 tablespoons grated Parmesan cheese (1½ ounces) (divided)

7 tablespoons unsalted butter, cold, cut into small pieces

½ cup heavy cream

1 large egg, beaten

Filling

1. Preheat the oven to 375°F. Butter a deep 9-by-13-inch baking dish.

2. In a large colander, combine the onions, peas, and corn. Let thaw while preparing the rest of the dish.

3. Melt 2 tablespoons of the butter in a frying pan over medium heat, add the carrots, and sauté until beginning to soften. Add the leeks and sauté about 3 minutes more.

4. Place the carrots and leeks into the colander with the defrosting vegetables.

5. Place the pan over high heat and add 1 tablespoon of the butter and ½ tablespoon of the oil. As soon as the foam from the butter starts to subside, meaning the pan is hot enough, add half of the mushrooms. Toss and shake the pan for 4 to 5 minutes. The mushrooms will first absorb the fat but in a few minutes the fat will reappear and the mushrooms will brown. Once they have browned, immediately remove them from the pan and repeat with the second half of mushrooms, 1 tablespoon of butter, and the remaining ½ tablespoon of oil.

6. Add the browned mushrooms, diced chicken, and vegetable mixture to a large bowl.

7. In a large saucepan over medium heat, melt the remaining 6 tablespoons of butter. Make a roux by sprinkling in the flour and cooking for about 3 minutes, stirring constantly. Slowly add the broth and half-and-half, whisking constantly, until the mixture is thickened and smooth. Season with the salt and pepper. Pour the sauce over the chicken-vegetable mixture. Add the parsley and dill and mix well. Taste and adjust the seasonings if needed.

8. Pour the mixture into the prepared dish.

Cobbler Dough

1. In a medium bowl, sift together the flour, baking powder, salt, and 3 tablespoons of Parmesan cheese.

2. With a pastry blender or your hands, cut in the butter until the mixture resembles coarse meal. Add the cream, a little at a time, stirring and tossing with a fork just until the dough holds together. Add a bit more cream if the dough seems too dry.

3. On a lightly floured work surface, roll the dough into a rectangle large enough to cover the top of the baking dish. Drape it around the rolling pin and carefully lay it over the dish, folding the edges under. Don't worry too much about how the crust looks; it is very forgiving. If freezing, wrap in plastic now.

4. If baking immediately, brush the dough with the beaten egg and sprinkle the remaining 3 tablespoons of Parmesan evenly over the top.

5. Place the dish on a baking sheet and bake until the crust is browned and the filling starts to bubble, about 30 minutes. Check often near the end of the cooking time. I once set off the fire alarm at my friend's house when I forgot to use a baking sheet and the filling oozed out onto the oven. Not one of my finer moments.

If making the cobbler the day before the event, do not top the dish with the pastry until serving day. This ensures the pastry doesn't absorb any of the filling. If freezing, move the cobbler to the refrigerator the night before the party. Right before baking, brush with the egg mixture and sprinkle with the cheese. Cook the cobbler on a baking sheet at 375°F and check it after 60 minutes. Watch for the filling to bubble and, depending on the baking dish, this could take up to 20 minutes longer. To ensure the filling is hot, insert an instant-read thermometer into the center and remove when the middle reaches 160°F. Also, watch the crust carefully; if it becomes brown early, cover the crust with foil.

This updated variation of the traditional Waldorf salad (circa 1896) holds a special place in my heart. Having discovered this Bon Appétit *recipe on the* Epicurious *website in 1999, it remained filed away in my recipe collection, largely forgotten, until I received a plea for help from my two sons. It was November of 2005, just months after the devastation of Hurricane Katrina, when my phone rang. My sons needed assistance in finding an appropriate dish to contribute to an outdoor Thanksgiving dinner hosted by their friends in the badly hit Bywater District of New Orleans.*

Eric, who lived just outside the French Quarter in New Orleans, survived the hurricane with all of his possessions intact. His brother Gordon, visiting from Miami, was also a survivor of many of the same hurricanes that year. Amid the rubble, unflappable New Orleans residents tried their best at normalcy, and my sons were part of it in their own small way with their food contribution. I scratched my head at their request, trying to think of something easy, portable, and delicious—and here you have it.

WALDORF SALAD

SERVES 8 to 12

⅔ cup dried tart cherries
1 cup boiling water
½ cup good quality-mayonnaise, such as Hellmann's
3 tablespoons sour cream
2 tablespoons fresh lemon juice
1 teaspoon granulated sugar
4 tart apples, cut into ½-inch cubes
1⅓ cups very thinly sliced celery
1⅓ cups halved red seedless grapes
Kosher salt and ground black pepper
1 bunch romaine lettuce
Sweet and Spicy Candied Pecans (page 74)

1. In a small bowl, soak the cherries in the water until softened, about 10 minutes, then drain.
2. Whisk the mayonnaise, sour cream, lemon juice, and sugar in a large bowl. Add the apples, celery, grapes, and soaked cherries. Toss well and season with salt and pepper.
3. Arrange the lettuce leaves on a platter and spoon the salad on top. Sprinkle with the candied pecans.

These pecans are essential to the success of the Waldorf Salad but also can be used as a topping for many dishes, both sweet and savory. This makes more than enough to top a salad. While leftovers are easy to store, most end up as the cook's snack.

SWEET AND SPICY CANDIED PECANS

MAKES 1½ cups

3 tablespoons light corn syrup
1½ tablespoons granulated sugar
¾ teaspoon kosher salt
¼ teaspoon ground black pepper
⅛ teaspoon cayenne pepper
1½ cups chopped pecans

1. Preheat the oven to 325°F. Line a rimmed baking sheet with parchment paper.
2. In a medium bowl, mix together the corn syrup, sugar, salt, pepper, and cayenne pepper.
3. Add the pecans and stir gently to coat. Transfer the pecans to the prepared baking sheet.
4. Bake the pecans for 5 minutes. Using a fork, stir the pecans to ensure even coating of the melted spice mixture. Continue baking until the pecans are golden and the coating bubbles, about 10 minutes. Watch carefully.
5. Transfer the hot mixture to a piece of aluminum foil set on the counter. Working quickly, separate the nuts with a fork. Cool.

Store in airtight container at room temperature. Can be made three days ahead.

To complement the rich chicken cobbler, serve this simple fresh tomato and cucumber salad. Prepare it early in the day but add the dressing just before serving.

FRESH TOMATO AND CUCUMBER SALAD

SERVES 8 to 12

2 pints cherry or grape tomatoes, halved

2 cucumbers, chopped (peel if using the thick-skinned variety)

1 bunch scallions, white and green parts, chopped

⅓ cup chopped herbs such as parsley, dill, chives, or basil

¾ cup feta cheese, crumbled (3 ounces)

Kosher salt and ground black pepper

¼ cup extra-virgin olive oil

1½ tablespoons red wine vinegar

1 teaspoon Dijon mustard

Pinch granulated sugar

1. In a large bowl, combine the tomatoes, cucumbers, scallions, herbs, and feta cheese. Season with salt and pepper.

2. In a small bowl, whisk together the oil, vinegar, mustard, and sugar. Pour over the salad and toss right before serving.

We all have them: family recipes that, no matter how humble, endure. My mother rarely baked, but when she did, this was her go-to cake. I hesitated including a cake with such pedestrian ingredients, but this is the ticket for a moist lemony cake without much fuss. My sister and I conducted an unofficial taste comparison between it and Maida Heatter's famous 62nd Street Lemon Cake, which I also make. Don't strike me down for heresy, but if it were not for the artificial yellow coloring of the lemon jello, I don't think we could have distinguished between the two cakes.

Options abound for presentation. A cream cheese lemon glaze drizzled over the cake is included for fancier party fare, but it's traditionally served on its own with a sprinkling of powdered sugar over the top. I've encased it in cream cheese icing for birthday parties and placed individual slices atop swirls of raspberry puree for dinner parties.

As a testament to the confidence I place in this recipe, I baked ninety-six lemon cupcakes in my son Eric's studio apartment before his wedding rehearsal dinner. Okay, I did go a little overboard there.

LEMON CAKE

MAKES 1 (10-inch) cake | EQUIPMENT: tube cake pan, pastry brush

Unsalted butter and all-purpose flour, for greasing
1 package classic yellow cake mix
4 large eggs
¾ cup water
¾ cup Wesson oil
1 (3-ounce) box lemon Jell-O
Grated zest of 1 lemon

Scant ½ cup fresh lemon juice (3 to 4 medium lemons) plus 3 tablespoons
⅓ cup granulated sugar
Powdered sugar or Lemon Cream Cheese Glaze (recipe follows)

1. Preheat the oven to 350°F. Butter a tube pan and dust with flour.

2. In a large bowl, combine the cake mix, eggs, water, oil, Jell-O, zest, and 3 tablespoons of lemon juice. Using an electric mixer, mix on medium speed until well combined, about 2 minutes. Transfer the batter to the prepared pan.

3. Bake for 1 hour, or until toothpick inserted in the cake comes out clean. Let the cake cool for 5 minutes and then turn the cake out onto a wire rack that sits atop a large piece of aluminum foil or wax paper.

4. Meanwhile, in a small bowl combine the remaining ½ cup of lemon juice and the sugar.

5. Brush the glaze over the hot cake until it is all absorbed.

6. Let the cake cool completely. Using a baking sheet or pancake turner, invert the cake onto a cake plate.

7. Dust the cake with powdered sugar or drizzle with Lemon Cream Cheese Glaze.

Lemon Cream Cheese Glaze

This glaze is especially good for quick breads or whenever you want to enhance the richness of a dessert.

MAKES about 1 cup   EQUIPMENT: food processor

3 ounces cream cheese, room temperature
¾ cup sifted powdered sugar
2 tablespoons fresh lemon juice
1 teaspoon grated lemon zest
1 teaspoon vanilla extract
¼ cup heavy cream

1. In in a food processor, mix together the cream cheese, powdered sugar, lemon juice, lemon zest, vanilla, and cream to make a smooth, thick but pourable glaze. Add a few drops more cream if it seems too thick.

2. Drizzle over the cake.

The glaze is best used as soon as it is made.

A mini serving of this rich pudding satisfies our chocolate cravings while leaving room for a small piece of lemon cake. The unsweetened whipped cream and the crunchy coconut complete the dessert. Your guests will be licking their spoons for more.

This recipe was adapted from Dorie Greenspan's Dark Chocolate Pudding recipe. The ingredients remain the same as hers, but the cooking methods are somewhat simplified and the presentation is my own.

DARK CHOCOLATE PUDDING WITH TOASTED COCONUT

MAKES 6 servings (5 ounces) or 12 mini servings (2.5 ounces)
EQUIPMENT: fine mesh strainer, microwave

- 2 tablespoons cornstarch
- 2 tablespoons unsweetened cocoa powder
- ¼ teaspoon kosher salt
- 1 large egg
- 2 large egg yolks
- 4 ounces semisweet or bittersweet chocolate, chopped
- 1½ cups whole milk
- ¾ cup heavy cream
- ⅓ cup granulated sugar
- 1 teaspoon vanilla extract
- 2 tablespoons unsalted butter, room temperature
- 1 cup heavy cream, whipped
- 1 cup sweetened shredded coconut, toasted (see tip on page 63)

1. Set out 6 small bowls or 12 mini serving dishes for the pudding. Place a fine mesh strainer over a medium bowl. Set aside until ready for straining.

2. Whisk the cornstarch, cocoa powder, and salt in a medium heatproof bowl. Add in the egg and egg yolks, whisking to combine. Set aside.

3. Melt the chocolate by microwaving at 20 second intervals. Stir after each interval. Set the warm chocolate aside.

4. Add the milk, cream, and sugar to a medium saucepan. While stirring, heat the mixture over medium heat until you see small bubbles form around the edge of the pan. Watch carefully.

5. Remove from the heat and stir a few tablespoons of the hot liquid into the egg cocoa mixture. While continuing to stir, slowly add about one-fourth of the hot mixture into the eggs. Pour the now warm eggs back into the pan.

6. Place the pan back over medium heat and continue to whisk. Cook for about 3 minutes, until the pudding is thick and you see the first bubble break the surface. Once this happens, cook while whisking vigorously for a full minute.

7. Strain the pudding into the prepared medium bowl. Whisk in the warm chocolate, vanilla, and butter.

8. Spoon the pudding into the individual cups and place plastic wrap directly on the surface. Refrigerate. Right before serving, place a teaspoon of whipped cream over the pudding and sprinkle with toasted coconut.

Ginger Grapefruit Sparklers

Peppermint Cranberry Mocktails

Red Fish, Blue Fish, Tuna Salad

Mad Hatter Cucumber Tea Sandwiches

Deviled Green Eggs and Ham

Mr. McGregor's Cakes
(The World's Best Carrot Cake)

In the Night Kitchen Bourbon Pecan Cookies

Make Ahead

Up to 2 weeks before: Make and freeze the cake layers or cupcakes for the carrot cake(s), bake and freeze the pecan cookies.

Day before: Make the syrup for the sparklers, make the hibiscus tea, defrost cake layers or cupcakes in the refrigerator.

Morning of: Make the filling for the tea sandwiches, make the tuna salad, prepare the icing and frost the cake.

Afternoon of: Make the deviled eggs, wash greens for the tuna salad, defrost the cookies at room temperature.

Last hour: Construct the tea sandwiches. Mix together the beverages.

BABY LIT SHOWER
(FAIRY TALES AND FANTASY SPELLS)

This menu is based on a baby shower which my sister and I held in honor of my daughter-in-law, Virginia. Her position as a librarian at the Arlington, Texas, library inspired the children's literature theme. Most of the guests were also library employees, so we all shared in a common love of books. Giggles and chatter enveloped the house as everyone participated in a guessing game involving quotes from famous children's stories while we munched on carrot cake inspired by Mr. McGregor's garden of *Peter Rabbit* fame and tea sandwiches from *Alice's Adventures in Wonderland's* Mad Hatter.

Children's books are referenced in the menu titles, but sans the titles, these recipes are good for any type of afternoon celebration.

A Martha Stewart recipe was my inspiration for these sparkers, but many variations proliferate on the internet. What's especially appealing is the option to add sparkling wine at the last minute. Served along side the Ginger Grapefruit Sparklers are Peppermint Cranberry Mocktails. Bright and not too sweet, they are a refreshing afternoon beverage.

GINGER GRAPEFRUIT SPARKLERS

SERVES 6 | EQUIPMENT: fine mesh strainer

- 1 (3-inch) piece fresh ginger, peeled and thinly sliced
- ¼ cup granulated sugar
- ¼ cup water
- ¼ cup honey
- 4 cups Ruby Red grapefruit juice
- 1 grapefruit, sliced, for garnish
- 1 (12-ounce) can club soda or sparkling wine

1. In a small saucepan over medium heat, combine the ginger, sugar, water, and honey. Heat until the sugar and honey are dissolved, about 2 minutes. Let cool.
2. With a fine mesh strainer, strain the cooled ginger syrup into a pitcher filled with grapefruit juice and stir.
3. To serve, divide the mixture into 6 glasses and fill with ice. Top with either club soda or sparkling wine and garnish with a grapefruit slice.

PEPPERMINT CRANBERRY MOCKTAILS

SERVES 8 | EQUIPMENT: fine mesh strainer

- 4 peppermint tea bags
- 2 cups boiling water
- 3 cups cranberry juice cocktail
- 3 cups ginger ale
- Mint sprigs, for garnish

1. Steep the tea bags in boiling water for 5 minutes. Discard the tea bags and pour the tea into a large pitcher to cool.
2. Mix in the cranberry juice cocktail.
3. When ready to serve, add the ginger ale and serve over ice. Garnish each glass with a mint sprig.

Tuna salad was one of the first recipes passed on to me by my mother. It wasn't until I was the innocent age of twenty-one and living in my first apartment that I realized how clueless I was about simple survival cooking. A quick phone call to my mother rescued me. From her I learned the transformative properties of mayonnaise, onions, and pickles when added to a simple can of tuna. The only change to her original ingredients is the addition of apple slivers, which I happened upon many years later in a seaside cafe in the Florida Keys.

For the baby shower, serve the tuna on a platter lined with lettuce along with assorted crackers. One can of tuna serves three, so multiply as needed for the party.

RED FISH, BLUE FISH, TUNA SALAD

SERVES 3

- 1 (5-ounce) can tuna (any variety), drained
- ¼ cup finely chopped celery
- ¼ cup chopped dill pickles
- ¼ cup finely chopped red or white onion
- ¼ cup thinly sliced then finely chopped apple
- ¼ cup finely chopped pecans (optional)
- ⅓ cup good-quality mayonnaise, such as Hellmann's
- Kosher salt and ground black pepper

1. In a medium bowl, combine the tuna, celery, pickles, onion, apple, and pecans (if using). Add the mayonnaise, one spoonful at a time, depending on whether your tuna was packed in oil or not, as you may need less.

2. Taste and add salt and pepper as needed. Serve.

Cucumber sandwiches can be as simple as thinly sliced salted cucumber and butter. For bolder flavors, break with tradition with this amped-up version that includes cream cheese, ginger, dill, and jalapeño. Grating the cucumber and squeezing out the water eliminates any soggy bottoms on your sandwiches. Plain white bread is traditional, but whole grain or any type of soft bread work just as well.

MAD HATTER CUCUMBER TEA SANDWICHES

MAKES 18 tiny sandwiches | EQUIPMENT: box grater

- 1 large cucumber
- 1 (16-ounce) package cream cheese, room temperature
- ½ cup finely diced red bell pepper
- 2 teaspoons peeled and grated fresh ginger
- 2 tablespoons finely chopped dill
- ½ teaspoon lemon juice
- 2 teaspoons seeded and finely diced jalapeño (optional)
- ½ teaspoon kosher salt
- ½ teaspoon ground black pepper
- 12 slices soft bread, crusts removed

1. Peel the cucumber, leaving a few strips of green on it for color. Grate the cucumber on to a paper towel using the large side of a box grater. Gather the towel in your hand and squeeze out the water. There will be a lot. Transfer the grated cucumber to a medium bowl.

2. Add the cream cheese, bell pepper, ginger, dill, lemon juice, jalapeño (if using), salt, and pepper and mix well. Taste and season with salt and pepper as needed. The filling can be made in advance but make the sandwiches within an hour or two of serving.

3. Spread a thick layer of filling over half of the bread slices. Top with the remaining bread slices and cut each sandwich into three horizontal pieces. Serve.

Once a staple of church suppers and potlucks, deviled eggs are back, dressed up and delicious. They are a cinch to make, aside from the dastardly task of peeling the eggs. I've yet to find the magic formula for easy peeling, though plunging them into an ice bath for 15 minutes after cooking sometimes helps. My best advice is to turn on some music, pour yourself a drink, and start peeling.

The green color, a nod to Dr. Seuss, comes from finely chopped parsley. Optionally, other flavorful meats such as crispy bacon or smoked brisket are good substitutes for the ham, or go vegetarian with no meat at all.

DEVILED GREEN EGGS AND HAM

MAKES 24 deviled eggs

12 large eggs
½ cup good-quality mayonnaise, such as Hellmann's
2 teaspoons Dijon mustard
½ teaspoon kosher salt
1 teaspoon apple cider vinegar
Pinch cayenne pepper
½ cup finely chopped smoked deli ham
Parsley, finely chopped, for garnish

1. Place the eggs into a large pan and cover with an inch of water. Bring to a boil over high heat, watching closely. As soon as they come to a boil, cover the pan and remove from the heat. Let sit for 12 minutes, then drain the hot water and plunge the eggs into a pan of ice water to stop the cooking.

2. After 15 minutes, peel the eggs and slice in half lengthwise. Scoop out the yolks into a medium bowl and mash with a fork. Mix in the mayonnaise, mustard, salt, vinegar, and cayenne pepper. Taste and adjust the seasonings if needed. Fill the egg white halves with the mixture and place the chopped ham on top. Sprinkle each egg with the parsley, then serve.

You may be skeptical of the superlative in the name of this cake but don't be put off: bake it yourself before passing judgement. To my knowledge, there is no better carrot cake in the world.

With few exceptions, the cookbooks that remain on my shelf after decades of cooking must have a least one knockout recipe. Nathalie Dupree's Matters of Taste, *earned its shelf space in my home with this cake. The cookbook was a 1993 Christmas present from an admirer who later became my husband. He bought it on a whim from a benefit at the PBS TV station, KERA, in Dallas. Little did either of us know, it held this treasure; both he and the book were keepers.*

It is traditionally made as a three-layer cake but is easily adapted into mini cupcakes, which are more suitable for snacking by Peter Rabbit in Mr. McGregor's garden. Warning: the recipe makes eighty-four tiny cupcakes, so if you don't want to bother with cuteness, just make the layer cake.

MR. MCGREGOR'S CAKES (THE WORLD'S BEST CARROT CAKE)

MAKES 1 (3-layer) cake or 84 mini cupcakes | EQUIPMENT: 3 (9-inch) cake pans or 4 mini cupcake pans with mini cupcake liners

- 1½ cups whole wheat flour
- ⅔ cup all-purpose flour, plus more for dusting
- 2 teaspoons baking soda
- 2 teaspoons ground cinnamon
- ½ teaspoon kosher salt
- ½ teaspoon ground nutmeg
- ¼ teaspoon ground ginger
- 1 cup granulated sugar
- 1 cup packed light or dark brown sugar
- 1 cup buttermilk
- ¾ cup vegetable oil
- 4 large eggs
- 1½ teaspoons vanilla extract
- 1 (1-pound) bag carrots, peeled and grated
- 1 (8-ounce) can crushed pineapple, drained
- 1 cup chopped pecans or walnuts
- 1 cup sweetened shredded coconut
- ½ cup chopped dried cherries
- Cream Cheese Frosting (recipe follows)

Baby Lit Shower

1. Preheat the oven to 350°F.

2. Grease three (9-inch) round cake pans with pan spray or butter and dust with flour. Line the bottoms with parchment paper or line four mini cupcake pans with mini cupcake liners.

3. In a medium bowl, sift together the two flours, baking soda, cinnamon, salt, nutmeg, and ginger. Mix to combine.

4. In a large bowl, mix together the granulated and brown sugars, the buttermilk, oil, eggs, and vanilla. Mix well.

5. Add the flour mixture, carrots, pineapple, nuts, coconut, and cherries. Stir just until blended. Transfer the batter to the prepared cake or cupcake pans.

6. For cake layers, bake for 30 minutes, or until a toothpick inserted in the center comes out clean. For mini cupcakes, bake for 12 minutes, or until a toothpick inserted in the center comes out clean.

7. For cakes layers, cool in the pans for 10 minutes, then loosen the cake layers by sliding a knife around the edges. Invert the pans onto a wire rack and cool completely.

8. For mini cupcakes, cool for 10 minutes, then remove the cupcakes with their liners from the pans and cool completely on a wire rack.

9. When the cakes are completely cooled, frost with cream cheese frosting. To frost the cake, place the bottom layer on the serving plate and cover with a thin layer of frosting. Repeat with the second layer and top with the final layer, covering the cake with the remaining frosting. To frost the mini cupcakes, use a piping bag with a star tip to place a generous dollop of frosting on each cupcake.

Cream Cheese Frosting

This is my go-to cream cheese frosting for cakes. Don't skip the orange zest as it helps balance the sweetness.

MAKES enough to fill and frost 3 (9-inch) cake layers | EQUIPMENT: electric mixer

- ½ cup (1 stick) unsalted butter, room temperature
- 1 (8-ounce) package cream cheese, room temperature
- 2 teaspoons grated orange zest
- 1 teaspoon vanilla extract
- 1 (16-ounce) box powdered sugar

1. In the bowl of a stand mixer fitted with the paddle attachment, or in a large bowl if using a hand-held mixer, cream together the butter and cream cheese until fluffy, 3 to 5 minutes.
2. Add the orange zest and vanilla.
3. Gradually beat in the powdered sugar until smooth.

To keep your serving plate clean while you ice the cake, place three narrow strips of wax paper partially under the bottom layer. After the cake is completely frosted carefully pull out the protective strips.

Rich in butter, loaded with pecans, and spiked with bourbon, these cookies check all the boxes. Indicative of their hotel kitchen origins, they are simple to prepare and abundant in quantity. I discovered them in the Austin American-Statesman *newspaper in 2017. Troy Knapp was the executive chef of the Austin Driskill Hotel at the time and submitted this recipe. Don't be surprised if you find yourself late at night foraging for just one more of these addicting cookies.*

IN THE NIGHT KITCHEN BOURBON PECAN COOKIES

MAKES 5 dozen cookies | EQUIPMENT: electric mixer

1½ cups (3 sticks) unsalted butter, room temperature
1¾ cups granulated sugar
2 large egg yolks
½ teaspoon vanilla extract
¼ cup bourbon
3 cups all-purpose flour
2 teaspoons sea salt
3 cups pecans, finely chopped

1. Preheat oven to 325°F. Line two baking sheets with parchment paper.
2. In a large bowl, with an electric mixer, cream together the butter and sugar until light and fluffy, 3 to 5 minutes.
3. Slowly mix in the egg yolks, one at a time, followed by the vanilla and bourbon.
4. Add the flour and salt, then the pecans, mixing well. The batter will be very thick.
5. Scoop small balls of dough onto the prepared baking sheets, spacing them 2 inches apart. A small ice-cream scoop makes for uniform cookies. Press each ball down slightly and bake until golden brown, 10 to 14 minutes.
6. Cool for 5 minutes on the baking sheets, then move to a wire rack to cool completely.

These cookies freeze well for up to a month in an airtight container.

Summer Bourbon Rickey

Naan

Beef Sliders with
Sweet and Sour Red Onions

Chicken Tikka Skewers

Watermelon Chaat

Cucumber Raita

Lemon Jasmine Rice Salad
or
Charlie Bird's Farro Salad

Frozen Lime Pie
or
Banana Cream Pudding

Make Ahead
Up to 2 weeks before: Make the lime pie and freeze.
Up to 3 days before: Make the rice salad and the pastry cream for the pudding.
1 day before: Make the riata, complete the pudding, marinate the chicken, prepare the red onions for the sliders.
Early in the day: Make the slider patties, make the chaat and the farro salad.
Up to 5 hours before cooking: Make the naan dough, mix the bourbon rickey.
Last hour: Preheat the grill, finish naan preparation, finish the riata, finish the rice salad, grill the naan and the meat.

BACKYARD GRILL

Backyard grilling is not a speciality of mine, but it is of my son, Eric. When I broached the subject of writing this cookbook, Eric offered his advice on this chapter. He sent me ingredients and measurements via text, and I translated them into recipes. When we were together, he taught me how to build a good charcoal fire and position the naan and the skewers so they would cook and not incinerate. And, just maybe, he learned from me how to document and measure ingredients; the jury is still out on that.

Eric is adventurous in his grilling, from smoking oysters to roasting a whole pig for his rehearsal dinner the day before his wedding. He catered my sixtieth birthday party using an inexpensive backyard grill that he transported from his home in New Orleans, along with his homemade pâté and pickles for a masterfully grilled banh mi sandwich.

This meal is Indian inspired. All three of my sons spent their formative high school years working at an iconic Indian restaurant in Dallas. I believe the spices permeated their psyches as these flavors get top billing in their homes. The naan, the chicken, and the beef are grilled, but everything else is cold and prepared ahead of time, leaving more time to spend with your guests and imbibing in a summer cocktail or a beer or two.

Charcoal Grilling Basics

You need a few basic barbecue techniques for success with grilling. During my testing, I used a charcoal grill, which requires a little more finesse than grilling on a propane grill, but either method gives good results. As with most things, the more I grill the better my results.

1. Use an inexpensive charcoal chimney starter to heat your charcoal.
2. Once the coals are mostly covered in ash, arrange the charcoal so you create a two-zone grilling area where the coals are spread on one side of the charcoal grate and the other side is empty. This gives you a direct high to medium-high fire for cooking and a resting area to either finish cooking with the lid closed or a warming area to escape the heat or any flare-ups.
3. Once your coals are hot, preheat the grill for 10 minutes with the cooking rack in place and the lid closed, then scrape the grill to knock off any charred bits. Using tongs, brush the hot grill with a paper towel soaked with oil to prevent sticking.

I find serving this refreshing drink improves the flavors of my grilling.

SUMMER BOURBON RICKEY

SERVES 1 | EQUIPMENT: cocktail shaker, highball glass

2 ounces bourbon
1 ounce simple syrup or agave nectar
1 ounce fresh lime juice

Sparkling water
Lime slice, for garnish

1. In a cocktail shaker, mix the bourbon, simple syrup, and lime juice with ice. *Note: Can be prepared without the ice earlier in the day and refrigerated.*

2. Strain into an ice-filled highball glass and top with sparkling water. Garnish with a lime slice.

Naan, a traditional Indian flatbread, is the cornerstone of this meal. You can always buy prepared naan at a grocery store if time and inclination are not on your side, but for adventurous cooks, the reward is worth the effort.

NAAN

MAKES 8 pieces | EQUIPMENT: pastry brush

- 1 (¼-ounce) packet active dry yeast
- 1 teaspoon granulated sugar
- ½ cup warm whole or 2% milk (about 15 seconds in the microwave, no more than 110°F)
- ½ cup warm water
- 4 cups all-purpose flour, plus more for dusting
- 1½ teaspoons kosher salt, plus more for sprinkling
- 1 teaspoon baking powder
- ¼ cup plain low-fat yogurt, room temperature
- 2 tablespoons vegetable oil or ghee, plus more for greasing
- Clarified unsalted butter (ghee), for brushing

1. In a small bowl, mix the sugar with the warm milk and water, then sprinkle the yeast over the mixture. After a minute or two, stir with a spoon or a fork to dissolve the yeast. Let it sit for another 5 minutes while you prepare the other ingredients. The mixture should form a few bubbles or foam, indicating the yeast is active.

2. In a large bowl, mix together 3 cups of the flour, the salt, and baking powder, then add in the yogurt, oil, and yeast mixture. Using one hand, mix the wet and dry ingredients together.

3. Turn the dough out onto a floured surface; it should come together into a ball. Knead the dough for about 5 minutes, until the surface becomes smooth, soft, and slightly sticky, adding more of the remaining 1 cup of flour as needed. (You may not use the whole cup).

4. Lightly grease the bowl with oil, place the dough in the bowl, and turn to coat. Cover the bowl with plastic wrap. Let the dough rise in a warm draft-free area until doubled in size, about 1 hour. *Note: Naan dough can be made up to 4 hours before cooking but should rest in the refrigerator after the first rise if you are preparing it early.*

5. With floured hands, punch down the dough. Let the dough rest for another 30 minutes. Heat the grill to medium-high heat.

6. Divide the dough into eight equal balls and, taking one piece at a time, stretch the dough with your hands or roll it out with a rolling pin to about a ¼-inch thickness. Pick up the dough by the top and stretch it into a teardrop shape. Place the dough on the grill and cook until lightly blistered, puffed, and cooked through, about 2 minutes. Flip it and cook on the other side until it is browned in patches. Watch carefully and adjust grill placement if the naan is cooking too quickly and burning; a little black is okay. Continue flipping until there are no doughy pieces remaining.

7. Brush with the clarified butter and sprinkle with salt. Wrap in foil to keep warm until ready to serve.

Alternatively, you can cook the naan in a heavy skillet over medium-high heat and follow the same instructions as for grilling. For garlic-chile naan, add 2 teaspoons of minced serrano chile, 2 teaspoons of minced garlic, and 2 teaspoons dried minced garlic to the yogurt flour mixture.

These are easy-to-prepare Asian-inspired ground beef sliders that pair well with the buttery naan and the cucumber raita. Topping them with the sweet and sour red onion mixture provides a well-balanced flavor profile. If doubling the recipe to make twelve sliders, there is no need to double the onion mixture. There are more than enough red onions for everyone.

BEEF SLIDERS WITH SWEET AND SOUR RED ONIONS

MAKES 6 (2-inch) patties | EQUIPMENT: grill tongs

Red Onions

1 tablespoon light or dark brown sugar
2 tablespoons white wine vinegar
Pinch kosher salt
1 small red onion, finely sliced

Sliders

1 pound 80% lean ground chuck
4 scallions, white part only, finely chopped
2 garlic cloves, minced
1 teaspoon sriracha
½ teaspoon kosher salt
¼ teaspoon grated peeled fresh ginger
1 tablespoon soy sauce
3 tablespoons roasted salted pumpkin seeds, coarsely chopped (optional)
Small handful finely chopped fresh cilantro leaves
Vegetable oil, for the grill

Red Onions

1. In a small bowl mix together the brown sugar, vinegar, and a pinch of salt. Add in the red onion. Leave the mixture to macerate while you prepare the ground meat. *Note: For milder onions, prepare them several hours before serving and chill in the refrigerator.*

Sliders

1. Place the ground meat in a large bowl and add the scallions, garlic, sriracha, salt, ginger, soy sauce, and pumpkin seeds (if using). Mix gently with a fork to combine, taking care not to compress the ingredients.

2. Lightly shape the meat into six patties. These can be prepared early in the day, covered, and refrigerated.

3. Let the patties come to room temperature while you prepare the gas or charcoal grill (see Charcoal Grilling Basics, page 96). When the grill is ready, add the

patties and cook over medium-high heat for 4 minutes. Flip the patties with a spatula and cook for another 4 minutes, depending on the temperature of your grill and the desired doneness. If you are unsure, test with an instant-read thermometer; 160°F is the safe temperature for ground beef.

4 Transfer the sliders to a platter and cover with aluminum foil until dinner time.

5 Add the cilantro to the red onion mixture and serve the red onions along side the sliders.

The chicken skewers cook quickly, so watch carefully and make sure to lightly oil the grill to prevent sticking. The longer the marinade time, the more the spices permeate the meat.

CHICKEN TIKKA SKEWERS

SERVES 4 | EQUIPMENT: barbecue skewers

1 cup plain yogurt
1 teaspoon chili powder
1 tablespoon minced garlic
1 tablespoon minced fresh ginger
1 teaspoon ground turmeric
1 tablespoon chopped fresh cilantro
1 teaspoon kosher salt
1 teaspoon ground paprika
1 tablespoon fresh lemon juice, plus more for finishing
1 tablespoon curry powder (optional)
1½ to 2 pounds skinless chicken tenders or chicken breasts, cut into 1½-inch pieces

1. In a resealable plastic bag, combine the yogurt, chili powder, garlic, ginger, turmeric, cilantro, salt, paprika, lemon juice and curry powder (if using). Add the chicken and turn to coat. Seal the bag and transfer to a baking dish. Refrigerate for a least 2 hours or up to 8 hours. Bring the chicken to room temperature before grilling. If using wooden skewers, soak them in cold water for a least 30 minutes prior to grilling.
2. Set up a gas or charcoal grill for medium high-heat. Heat to 400°F (see Charcoal Grilling Basics, page 96).
3. Remove the chicken from the marinade and scrape off any excess.
4. Thread the chicken onto skewers.
5. Grill over medium-high heat for 2 to 3 minutes per side, until the juices run clear when pierced with the tip of a fork and the chicken is no longer pink. If you are unsure, test with an instant-read thermometer; 160°F is the safe temperature for chicken. After each skewer browns, move to the cool side of grill while the others cook. Finish with a squeeze of lemon juice.

There are many wonderful ways to serve watermelon during the summer, but this recipe with its slight kick of jalapeño is both unexpected and refreshing. An Indian "chaat" is a loosely defined dish, but in general, it's a snack that is sweet, sour, tangy, spicy, and crunchy. If watermelon is not in season, you can substitute cubed apple or pear, or whatever is readily available for a satisfying fruity side dish. The was inspired by a recipe, published in the New York Times, *and adapted by Tejal Rao.*

WATERMELON CHAAT

SERVES 6 | EQUIPMENT: spice mill or mortar and pestle

8 cups 1-inch cubed watermelon
1 teaspoon whole cumin seeds
½ teaspoon sweet paprika
¼ teaspoon finely ground black pepper
Pinch ground cayenne pepper
½ teaspoon fine sea salt

⅓ cup fresh orange juice
¾ teaspoon finely chopped jalapeño (optional)
5 to 6 fresh mint leaves, thinly sliced
¼ cup roasted salted sunflower kernels (optional)

1. Place the cubed watermelon in a large serving bowl.
2. Toast the cumin seeds in a small dry skillet over medium heat until deep brown, 2 to 3 minutes. Grind the seeds in a spice mill or pound with a mortar and pestle.
3. In a small bowl combine the cumin, paprika, black pepper, cayenne, salt, orange juice, and jalapeño (if using). Pour over the watermelon. Can be made early in the day.
4. Right before serving, add in the fresh mint leaves and sprinkle with sunflower kernels, if using. Taste and add more salt if needed.

A cucumber raita is the perfect accompaniment to a grilled meal, especially when Indian spices are featured. It's good on top of the chicken tikka or spread over the naan; really it's welcome with all the flavors on your plate.

Using a Microplane to grate the garlic gives the raita a punch of flavor without overpowering it.

CUCUMBER RAITA

MAKES 4 to 6 servings | EQUIPMENT: Microplane, spice mill or mortar and pestle, box grater

1 teaspoon whole cumin seeds
½ large cucumber
1 cup plain full-fat yogurt
1 large garlic clove, grated
1 teaspoon chopped fresh cilantro
1 teaspoon chopped fresh mint
½ teaspoon minced seeded jalapeño
2 teaspoons fresh lemon juice, or more as needed
1 teaspoon kosher salt, or more as needed
Ground black pepper

1. Toast the cumin seeds in a small dry skillet over medium heat until deep brown, 2 to 3 minutes. Grind the seeds in a spice mill or pound with a mortar and pestle.

2. Peel the cucumber, leaving a few strips of green for color. Grate the cucumber on to a paper towel using the large side of a box grater. Gather the towel in your hand and squeeze out the water, there will be a lot. Transfer the grated cucumber to a medium bowl.

3. Add the yogurt, cumin, garlic, cilantro, mint, jalapeño, lemon juice, and salt. Taste and season with salt, pepper, and lemon juice if needed.

The raita can be made the day before and refrigerated, but add the cilantro and the mint the day of the meal.

Lemon and fresh herbs give this cold rice salad a freshness that is in keeping with the theme of summer grilling.

LEMON JASMINE RICE SALAD

SERVES 6

- 2 tablespoons extra-virgin olive oil (divided)
- ¼ cup minced shallots
- 1 cup jasmine or basmati rice
- 2 cups vegetable or chicken stock
- 1 teaspoon kosher salt
- 1 small red bell pepper, finely chopped
- ½ cup finely chopped red onion, rinsed in cold water
- ½ cup chopped fresh herbs such as parsley, basil, or mint
- ½ cup coarsely chopped salted roasted almonds
- 1 teaspoon grated lemon zest
- 2½ teaspoons fresh lemon juice
- Ground black pepper

1. In a medium saucepan over medium heat, heat 1 tablespoon of the oil until shimmering. Add the shallots and cook until soft but not brown, about 3 minutes. Add the rice and continue to sauté for about 2 minutes longer, stirring regularly.

2. Add the stock and salt and bring to a boil. Reduce the heat to low, cover, and simmer until all the liquid is absorbed, 14 to 16 minutes.

3. Remove from the heat and let stand, partially covered, for 5 minutes. Fluff the rice with a fork and pour into a large bowl to cool completely.

4. In a small bowl, mix together the bell pepper, onion, herbs, nuts, lemon zest, lemon juice, and remaining 1 tablespoon of oil. Add to the cooled rice and gently stir to combine. Add pepper to taste.

This salad keeps for three days covered in the refrigerator. If making ahead of time, add the herbs the day of the meal.

This dish, from the Charlie Bird restaurant in Soho, features the ancient wheat grain known as farro. Similar but, in my opinion, better than brown rice. It is nutty, chewy, and a perfect foil for the lemony vegetables in this dish.

Farro is sold either as whole grain, pearled (perlato), or semi-pearled (semi-pearlato). If you can find it, use semi-pearled for this recipe as it only takes 30 minutes to cook.

CHARLIE BIRD'S FARRO SALAD

SERVES 6 to 8

1 cup semi-pearled farro
1 cup apple cider
2 bay leaves
2 teaspoons kosher salt (divided)
2 cups water
½ cup extra-virgin olive oil
¼ cup fresh lemon juice
½ teaspoon ground black pepper

½ cup chopped roasted salted pistachios
1 cup chopped parsley
1 cup chopped fresh mint leaves
1 cup halved cherry tomatoes
⅓ cup thinly sliced radishes
2 cups baby arugula
½ cup shaved Parmesan cheese
Pinch flaky sea salt

1. In a medium saucepan, combine the farro, apple cider, bay leaves, 1 teaspoon of the salt, and the water. Bring to a boil over high heat, then reduce the heat to low and simmer, uncovered, for about 30 minutes. If all the liquid is absorbed before the farro is tender, add a little more water. When the farro is tender, drain the liquid, remove and discard the bay leaves, and transfer to a serving bowl to cool.

2. In a small cup, whisk together the oil, lemon juice, remaining 1 teaspoon of salt, and the pepper. Stir the mixture into the warm farro and let cool for at least 15 minutes.

3. Close to serving time, stir in the pistachios, parsley, mint, tomatoes, and radishes. Add the arugula and lightly fold in the Parmesan so it retains its shape. Sprinkle with the sea salt, then serve.

I've made this hours ahead of dinner, as well as brought it to a potluck, and it always holds up well.

My sister, Fran, developed this traditional lime pie recipe. The technique is simple, but the contrasting flavors of the tart lime and the sweet, rich cream is complex. The frozen confection is perfect for a hot outdoor event.

FROZEN LIME PIE

SERVES 8 to 10 | EQUIPMENT: 9-inch pie plate, food processor, electric mixer

Crust

7 graham crackers, broken into small pieces

¾ cup sliced or slivered almonds or pecans

¼ cup granulated sugar

4 tablespoons unsalted butter, melted

Filling

2 (14-ounce) cans sweetened condensed milk

Grated zest of 2 limes

1 cup fresh lime juice (6 to 8 limes)

6 large egg yolks

Decoration

1 cup heavy cream, cold

¼ cup granulated sugar

¼ teaspoon vanilla extract

Crust

1. Preheat the oven to 350°F.
2. In a food processor, pulse together the graham crackers, almonds, and sugar until finely ground. Pour in the butter and pulse a few times just to combine.
3. Press the crumb mixture evenly onto the bottom and sides of a pie plate. Bake until lightly browned, 8 to 10 minutes. Cool completely.

Filling

1. In a large bowl, gently whisk together the condensed milk, lime zest, lime juice, and egg yolks until smooth. Pour into the baked crust and bake just until the center is set, 15 to 20 minutes.
2. Cool completely (filling will set as it cools).

Decoration

1. In a large bowl, beat the heavy cream on high speed of an electric mixer fitted with the whisk attachment until soft peaks form. Add the sugar and vanilla and beat until firm. Spoon or pipe the cream onto the pie. Freeze for several hours or overnight. Remove from the freezer 5 to 10 minutes before serving.

This pudding is large and luscious. I've served it many times, and even after a full night of eating and drinking, this dessert is never refused and dessert plates are licked clean.

BANANA CREAM PUDDING

SERVES 8 to 12 | EQUIPMENT: wire rack

1 (11-ounce) box vanilla wafers

Vanilla Pastry Cream (recipe follows), chilled

6 large bananas, sliced into ¼-inch coins

Marshmallow Meringue (recipe follows)

1. Cover the bottom of a 7-by-11-inch or 9-inch square baking dish, glass or ceramic, with a layer of vanilla wafers.
2. Spread half of the pastry cream over the wafers.
3. Tile three of the bananas over the cream. Repeat with another layer of wafers (you'll use half to three-fourths of the box in total), the remainder of the pastry cream, and the remaining three bananas.
4. Cover with plastic wrap and refrigerate until ready to top with the meringue.
5. Preheat the oven to 375°F.
6. Top the prepared pudding mixture with the marshmallow meringue so it touches the baking dish and seals the mixture. Use the back of the spoon to swirl the meringue into decorative swoops. Place on a wire rack atop a rimmed baking sheet in the lower-middle portion of the oven.
7. Bake until the meringue is browned all over, about 5 to 10 minutes, watching carefully. Cool for 1 hour at room temperature, then cover loosely with plastic and refrigerate until cold, about 1 hour more.

Vanilla Pastry Cream

Pastry cream, which is just a thick, rich pudding, is easy to make as long as you understand the essentials of tempering eggs. Tempering is combining hot liquid with an egg mixture without scrambling the eggs. Follow the instructions carefully and you won't have any issues.

MAKES 4 cups | EQUIPMENT: fine mesh strainer

1 large egg plus 4 large egg yolks

½ cup granulated sugar

3 tablespoons cornstarch

¼ teaspoon kosher salt

3 cups whole milk

1 teaspoon vanilla extract

6 tablespoons unsalted butter, cut into 6 slices, room temperature

1. Fill a large bowl with ice cubes and a little cold water. Place a heatproof bowl on top of the ice cubes. Place a fine mesh strainer over the bowl. Set aside.

2. In another large bowl, whisk together the egg and yolks, sugar, cornstarch, and salt.

3. In a large saucepan over medium-low heat, gently warm the milk until it just simmers. Remove from the heat.

4. While whisking, ladle about ½ cup of the hot milk into the egg mixture. Continue to slowly add the remaining milk to the eggs, whisking constantly.

5. Return the mixture to the saucepan and cook over medium heat while carefully stirring and scraping the bottom of the pan to prevent burning. When the custard has thickened and bubbles appear on the top of the pan, about 3 minutes, boil for 1 full minute, continuing to whisk. The custard needs to cook long enough or it will be pasty, but not too long or it will separate. It's not as finicky as it sounds; just watch the time.

6. Remove from the heat and pour the mixture through the strainer into the bowl on top of the ice cubes. Add the vanilla and stir in the butter until it is incorporated.

7. Cover the pastry cream with plastic wrap, pressing it gently on top of the mixture to prevent skin from forming. When the bowl feels cool to the touch, move it to the refrigerator where it will keep for up to 3 days.

Marshmallow Meringue

The beauty of this meringue is that it is substantial and won't weep or collapse. You can make this with a hand-held mixer if a stand mixer is not handy, but beating is a little more tedious.

MAKES 4 cups | EQUIPMENT: stand mixer, digital thermometer

4 large egg whites
¾ cup granulated sugar
¼ teaspoon kosher salt
⅛ teaspoon cream of tartar
½ teaspoon vanilla extract (optional)

1. In the bowl of a stand mixer, stir together the egg whites, sugar, salt, and cream of tartar.

2. Set the bowl over a pot that is slightly larger than your bowl and is filled with 1½ to 2 inches of simmering water. The water should just barely touch the bottom of the bowl. Turn the heat to low.

3. Stir and scrape constantly with a flexible spatula until the mixture is thin, foamy, and 175°F on a digital thermometer, about 10 minutes.

4. Transfer the bowl to the stand mixer fitted with the whisk attachment, add vanilla (if using), and whip on high until glossy, thick, and quadrupled in volume, about 5 minutes. Use immediately.

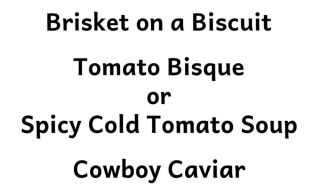

Brisket on a Biscuit

**Tomato Bisque
or
Spicy Cold Tomato Soup**

Cowboy Caviar

Fresh Grapes or Sliced Fruit

Mixed Fruit Crisp with Almonds

Midnight Chocolate Cake with Orange-Lemon Curd Filling

Make Ahead

Up to a 2 weeks before: Make the biscuits and freeze.
Up to a week before: Bake the chocolate cake and freeze. Make the curd, the sugared pecans, and the toasted almonds for the fruit crisp.
1 day before: Make the bisque or soup. Make the Cowboy Caviar minus the tomatoes and cilantro. Defrost the frozen cake in the refrigerator.
Day of: Make the ganache and assemble the cake. Make the fruit crisp.
An hour before: Bake and assemble the biscuits. Heat the bisque. Add the tomatoes and cilantro to the Cowboy Caviar.

BOOK CLUB

Book clubs have a long history in the United States. Analytical discussion groups date back to as early as 1634 when in the Massachusetts Bay Colony a religious renegade, Anne Hutchinson, began the tradition. Today book club membership is estimated in the United States at more than five million.

I'm a relative newbie to book clubs. In 2014, a friend and I established the neighborhood Shores Book Club, which has been a phenomenal success. Our meetings always include wine, appetizers and, though I wouldn't call us renegades, lively discussions. Depending on the host and the book, the food reflects in some small way the themes or locale of the book. This chapter does not feature a particular book, but is a sampling of some of the recipes prepared for my book club meetings. Think of serving Cowboy Caviar with a discussion of *Lonesome Dove,* or Mixed Fruit Crisp with Almonds while debating morality in *Where the Crawdads Sing*. Whatever the book, these recipes are especially good when paired with wine and stimulating conversation.

My sister, Fran Woodfin, developed this recipe for these finger-licking gems. Patina Green, a small farm-to-table lunch spot in McKinney, Texas, inspired the combination of biscuit and brisket. Fran and I experimented with many different biscuit recipes. The one I've settled on is based on Stella Parks's biscuit recipe from her cookbook BraveTart. *This recipe makes eight biscuits, so depending on the size of your gathering, you may want to make smaller biscuits or two batches.*

Sandwiched between the split biscuit is a jalapeño jelly or jam and chopped brisket. I've used many varieties of jalapeño jelly; my favorite has added fruit. Look for something that is sweet and hot. You can cook your own brisket, but I usually buy it from a local restaurant.

These biscuits include smoked cheddar cheese, which complements the smoky brisket and spicy jalapeño. Omit the cheese and you have a traditional breakfast biscuit ready for your favorite fruit preserves or honey.

BRISKET ON A BISCUIT

MAKES 8 (2½-inch) biscuits | EQUIPMENT: 2½-inch biscuit cutter, 8-inch metal cake pan or cast-iron skillet

- 2 cups all-purpose flour (9 ounces), plus more for rolling
- 1 tablespoon baking powder
- 2 teaspoons granulated sugar
- 1½ teaspoons kosher salt
- 6 tablespoons unsalted butter, cold, cut into ½-inch cubes
- ½ cup grated smoked cheddar cheese (2 ounces)
- ¾ cup buttermilk plus 2 tablespoons
- ½ cup jalapeño jelly (with fruit)
- 1 pound chopped brisket

1. Preheat the oven to 400°F. Adjust the oven rack to the lower-middle position.
2. The secret to this recipe is keeping everything cold and working quickly. Sift the flour into a large bowl, then whisk in the baking powder, sugar, and salt.
3. Drop the butter slices into the bowl and quickly toss to coat with flour. With floured fingers, lightly smash each butter cube into a flat size piece. Work quickly and don't worry about precision. Add the cheese and stir.

4. Add the ¾ cup of buttermilk to the flour. Stir briskly with a fork until a ball forms with no dry flour bits. Add the remaining 2 tablespoons of buttermilk if the mixture seems too dry. The dough should be sticky and shaggy but clear the sides of the bowl.

5. With floured hands, bring the dough together into a cohesive ball and transfer to a lightly floured counter. Dust the surface of the dough lightly with flour and pat into an approximate 6-inch square. Fold in half, then repeat, patting into a square and folding in half two more times.

6. Pat or roll the dough until it is ¾ inch thick and cut out as many 2½-inch rounds as you can. When cutting the dough, cut straight down and do not twist. Arrange the biscuits in an 8-inch metal cake pan with the sides touching. Gather together any scraps and cut out a few more biscuits. Leftovers are for the cook. If making ahead, stop now, cover and wrap the cut-out biscuit dough and freeze for up to a month. When ready to bake, continue with step 7 and watch the biscuits carefully to prevent burning.

7. Bake in the lower middle of the oven until the tops are golden brown and crisp, 30 to 35 minutes.

8. To assemble, slit the biscuits in the half and spread one side with the jelly and the other side with chopped brisket. Serve like a small hand-held sandwich.

These can also be made into smaller servings by using a 2-inch biscuit cutter.

In the early 1980s, which seems like a lifetime ago, I received this recipe from a chef at a Holiday Inn in Portland, Oregon. My former husband spent an extended period of time working at this hotel, and it was a daily favorite of his. At the end of his visit, he asked for the recipe so that I could re-create if for him at home. The chef's faded, tomato-splotched yellow legal pad paper, scribbled on in pencil, remains in my stash of recipes.

This is an old-fashioned creamy, rich soup, so for the book club I suggest serving it in small teacups along side the Brisket on a Biscuit. Six ounces fits into a standard teacup. The flavor improves with time, so prepare it the day before it is served.

TOMATO BISQUE

SERVES 12 (6-ounce servings)　|　EQUIPMENT: electric blender or food processor, immersion blender (optional)

6 tablespoons unsalted butter (divided)
1 small onion, diced
2 celery stalks, diced
1 (28-ounce) can whole tomatoes, chopped in a blender or food processor
2 (6-ounce) cans tomato paste
2 cups chicken or vegetable stock
½ teaspoon dried minced garlic

1 tablespoon granulated sugar, plus more if needed
Pinch ground cloves
1 teaspoon table salt
½ teaspoon ground black pepper
2 tablespoons all-purpose flour
1 (12-ounce) can evaporated milk
Parsley, for garnish

1 In a large pot, over medium heat, melt 1 tablespoon of the butter until it foams. Add the onion and celery and cook, stirring, for 3 to 5 minutes, until the vegetables are soft. Add the tomatoes, tomato paste, chicken stock, garlic, sugar, cloves, salt, and pepper. Turn the heat up to medium-high and bring the mixture to a boil, then reduce the heat to low and simmer, partially covered, for 20 minutes.

2 While the soup is simmering, prepare a light roux by melting 2 tablespoons of the butter in a small saucepan over medium heat. Add the flour and cook, stirring constantly, for 2 to 3 minutes. The roux should puff slightly and just begin to color. Let the roux cool to warm before adding it to the soup.

3. Add the warm roux to the soup and heat over medium heat, stirring constantly to incorporate. Partially cover and simmer again for another 20 minutes. Stir occasionally.

4. While the mixture cooks, heat the milk in a small saucepan over medium heat until almost boiling.

5. After the soup has cooked, slowly add in the hot milk, whipping continuously. Simmer the soup on low for 5 minutes.

6. Whip in the remaining 3 tablespoons of butter until fully incorporated. Taste and adjust seasonings if needed. Garnish with parsley.

If you want a less chunky soup, use a immersion blender to puree the mixture after it cools. Can be made the day before and heated right before serving.

An alternative to the warm creamy tomato bisque is this cold spicy soup, appropriate for a summer book club meeting. Adapted from a Bon Appétit *article from 1999, it's a refreshing change from gazpacho. If you don't have access to flavorful fresh tomatoes, I find that canned chopped tomatoes also work very well and make the soup even easier to prepare.*

SPICY COLD TOMATO SOUP

SERVES 6 | EQUIPMENT: electric blender

Soup

2 tablespoons extra-virgin olive oil
6 scallions, white part only, chopped
1 red bell pepper, chopped
2 garlic cloves, chopped
1 small jalapeño, seeded and chopped
4 cups tomato juice
1½ pounds tomatoes, peeled and chopped, or 1 (24-ounce) can chopped tomatoes
3 tablespoons fresh lime juice
1 teaspoon granulated sugar
½ teaspoon kosher salt
2 tablespoons prepared horseradish

Chipotle Cream

¼ cup sour cream
1 tablespoon minced seeded canned chipotle chiles
2 teaspoons fresh lime juice
¼ cup heavy cream
Kosher salt and ground black pepper

Soup

1. Heat the oil in a heavy large saucepan over low heat until shimmering. Add the scallions, bell pepper, garlic, and jalapeño. Cover and cook for about 10 minutes, until vegetables are tender, stirring often.

2. Add the tomato juice, tomatoes, lime juice, sugar, salt, and horseradish. Increase the heat to medium high and boil, uncovered, for about 10 minutes.

3. Cool slightly. Working in batches, puree the soup in a blender until smooth. Season with salt and pepper and add more sugar if the mixture tastes too acidic. Chill for at least 4 hours or overnight.

Chipotle Cream

1. Mix sour cream, chiles, and lime juice in a medium bowl. Gradually whisk in the heavy cream. Season with salt and pepper.

2. To serve, divide the soup into cups and offer the chipotle cream on the side.

To easily peel fresh tomatoes, start by bringing a large pot of water to boil over high heat. Make a shallow X on the bottom of each tomato and drop them into boiling water for 1 minute. Watch carefully and, using a slotted spoon, immediately remove the tomatoes, then plunge them into ice water. The skins should slide off. Set aside.

For a low sodium option that does not sacrifice flavor, substitute low sodium vegetable juice for the tomato juice.

This recipe has staying power. Created in 1940 by Helen Corbitt, the culinary director of Neiman Marcus in Dallas, this savory combination remains popular today. It is traditionally made with black-eyed peas, but I enjoy it best made with black beans or chickpeas. Use this recipe as a blueprint, adding and subtracting ingredients, and let the season be your guide. The main rule is to incorporate some type of bean into the dish; canned are fine, but always make your own vinaigrette dressing. Dorie Greenspan's recipe from Everyday Dorie *inspired this rendition.*

COWBOY CAVIAR

SERVES 4 as a side dish or 8 as a dip | EQUIPMENT: Microplane

- ¼ cup extra-virgin olive oil
- Grated zest and juice of 1 lime
- 1 teaspoon ground cumin
- ¾ teaspoon kosher salt
- ½ teaspoon smoked paprika
- ½ teaspoon honey
- 1 (15-ounce) can beans (black, pinto, black-eyed peas, chickpeas), drained
- ½ cup thawed frozen corn or sautéed fresh corn
- 4 scallions, white and green parts, thinly sliced
- 1 garlic clove, minced or grated
- ½ cup finely chopped red onion, rinsed in cold water
- ½ cup finely chopped red bell pepper
- 1 teaspoon seeded and finely chopped jalapeño
- 3 medium tomatoes, finely chopped, or 1 (14½-ounce) can of fire-roasted diced tomatoes, drained
- ½ cup finely chopped fresh cilantro
- Hot sauce, for serving (optional)
- Tortilla chips, for serving

1. In a small bowl, whisk together the oil, lime zest and juice, cumin, salt, paprika, and honey. Set aside. May be made the day before and refrigerated.

2. Drain and rinse the canned beans.

3. In a medium bowl, mix together the beans, corn, scallions, garlic, onion, bell pepper, and jalapeño. Toss about three-fourths of the dressing with the vegetable mixture. Refrigerate for up to 1 day.

4. When ready to serve, add the tomatoes and cilantro. Taste and add all or part of the remaining dressing. You may want to add a little extra lime juice and if you want more heat, add hot sauce (if using). Serve with tortilla chips.

This recipe is adapted from Food52's, Genius Desserts. *I've made it many times with different types of berries, peaches, cherries, whatever looks freshest at the store. It's more of a guideline than a recipe. This was the most requested dish of all the goodies on the table when I served it at book club. It also gets top billing in the effort versus reward category.*

MIXED FRUIT CRISP WITH ALMONDS

SERVES 8 to 10 | EQUIPMENT: food processor

Unsalted butter, for greasing pan

2½ pounds blueberries (or fruit of choice)

1 cup raspberries

2 tablespoons freshly squeezed orange juice

½ cup granulated sugar, or to taste (depending on your fruit)

2 tablespoons cornstarch

1½ cups all-purpose flour

1½ cups lightly packed light brown sugar

Pinch kosher salt

¾ cup (1½ sticks) unsalted butter, very cold, cut into ½-inch cubes

1 cup sliced almonds or pecans, toasted

Whipped cream or vanilla ice cream, for serving (optional)

1. Heat the oven to 375°F. Butter a 9-by-13-inch or similar baking dish.

2. In a large bowl, combine the blueberries, raspberries, and orange juice and gently stir. Taste the fruit and add the sugar to taste. Add the cornstarch and gently mix.

3. In a food processor, pulse the flour, brown sugar, and salt to combine. Scatter the butter over the dry ingredients and pulse again, just enough for a crumb mixture to form. The mixture should hold together when pinched with your fingers.

4. Empty the mixture into a medium bowl and stir in the almonds. *Note: This can be made a day ahead and refrigerated.*

5. Empty the fruit mixture into the prepared pan and spread in an even layer. Gather up handfuls of the crumb mixture and press into rough chunks. Don't worry too much about the size. Scatter the chunks evenly over the fruit.

6. Bake for 40 to 45 minutes, or until the filling is bubbling at the edges. Watch carefully and rotate the pan halfway for even browning.

7 Let the crisp cool slightly on a wire rack. Serve either warm or at room temperature. For a party, I like to serve whipped cream alongside as it doesn't melt like ice-cream does, but should you have any leftovers, vanilla ice-cream is also a great option.

Sweet, tart, and crunchy, this combination hits all the notes. The cake without the frosting and filling was adapted from Simple Cake *by Odette Williams, which was featured in the* Wall Street Journal *in 2020. I've added my favorite flavors to this moist chocolate cake, a tart filling and a bittersweet chocolate topping.*

MIDNIGHT CHOCOLATE CAKE WITH ORANGE-LEMON CURD FILLING

MAKES 1 (9-inch) cake | EQUIPMENT: 9-inch square cake pan, Microplane

1¾ cups all-purpose flour, plus more for dusting

½ cup unsweetened Dutch-process cocoa powder

1½ teaspoons baking powder

1½ teaspoons baking soda

½ teaspoon kosher salt

1½ cups granulated sugar

2 large eggs, room temperature

1 cup whole milk

½ cup neutral oil, such as safflower oil

½ teaspoon vanilla extract

1 cup boiling water

Orange-Lemon Curd (recipe follows)

¼ cup Chocolate Ganache (page 59)

Sugared Pecans (recipe follows)

1. Preheat the oven to 350°F. Grease a 9-inch square cake pan with pan spray or butter and dust with flour, then line the bottom with parchment paper.

2. In a medium bowl, sift the flour, cocoa, baking powder, baking soda, and salt. Whisk in the sugar. Set aside.

3. In a large bowl, whisk together the eggs, milk, oil, and vanilla. Gradually add the flour mixture and whisk until there are no lumps. Stir in the boiling water.

4. Pour the batter into the prepared pan and bake 40 to 50 minutes. Start checking the cake at 40 minutes. A toothpick inserted in the center should come out clean and the cake should bounce back when lightly pressed.

5. Let the cake cool for 10 minutes, then run a knife around the cake to gently release the parchment paper. Flip the cake onto a wire rack and remove the bottom piece of parchment. If freezing, wrap the cooled cake tightly in plastic.

6. When the cake is completely cool, use a long serrated knife to slice it horizontally. Spread the curd filling on the bottom layer, then replace the top layer. Ice the top with the ganache and sprinkle with sugared pecans. To serve, use a knife with a thin blade and score a line across the top of the cake, dividing it in half, then score

another line perpendicular to that one, dividing it into quarters. Continue dividing each quadrant into equal pieces until you have 16 squares. Cut through the scored slices completely, then serve.

Orange-Lemon Curd Filling

This filling balances out very sweet desserts, especially chocolate ones, as well as being good on its own, slathered on a warm biscuit or mixed into yogurt.

MAKES 1 cup |EQUIPMENT: fine mesh strainer

3 large eggs, room temperature
½ cup granulated sugar
3 tablespoons fresh orange juice (1 large orange)
3 tablespoons fresh lemon juice (2 medium lemons)
4 tablespoons unsalted butter, cut into small pieces, room temperature
Grated zest of 1 large orange
Grated zest of 1 medium lemon

1. In a medium stainless steel bowl, whisk together the eggs, sugar, orange and lemon juice. Place the bowl over a saucepan filled with simmering water. *Note: The simmering water should not quite touch the bottom of the bowl.*
2. Cook over low heat, stirring constantly with a flexible spatula until the mixture is thick enough to coat the back of a spoon, about 10 minutes.
3. Remove from the heat, and if needed pour through a fine mesh strainer to remove any lumps, then stir in the butter and orange and lemon zest.
4. Pour the curd into a heatproof bowl. Press a piece of plastic wrap onto the top of the curd to prevent a skin from forming. Refrigerate until cool; the curd thickens as it cools.

The curd can be refrigerated for a week. When ready to use, remove from the refrigerator and let warm to room temperature for easier spreading.

Sugared Pecans

This is such a simple recipe, it hardly seems worth the trouble, but try it once and you'll be a convert. The scant sugar coating, along with the flavor of the toasted pecans, is worth the extra step. Try them atop vanilla ice cream with a little chocolate syrup and you've got an instant dessert.

MAKES 1 cup

1 tablespoon water
1 tablespoon granulated sugar

1 cup chopped pecans

1. Preheat the oven to 325°F. Line a rimmed baking sheet with parchment paper.
2. In a small skillet over medium-high heat, heat the water and sugar just until boiling. Remove from the heat and stir in the pecans to coat.
3. Spread the pecans on the prepared sheet and bake for 12 minutes, stirring after the first 6 minutes and watching closely. Remove from the oven when golden brown and cool to room temperature.

Store in an airtight container for up to a week.

Barcelona Sangria

Assorted Cheese and Cracker Tray

Mexican-Style Meatball Soup

Tamales

Bibb Lettuce and Orange Salad

Bourbon Walnut Pie

Oma's Molasses Cookies

Make Ahead
<u>Up to 3 weeks before:</u> Make the cookies.
<u>Up to 2 days before:</u> Make the pie crust and refrigerate.
<u>Day before:</u> Make the soup and refrigerate.
<u>Morning of:</u> Prep the salad ingredients, prepare the pie.
<u>Last hour:</u> Reheat the soup and the tamales. Assemble the salad and make the sangria.

CHRISTMAS EVE

During my childhood, Christmas tradition had Santa stop at our home first, making Christmas Eve the time of magic. As darkness fell, my brother, much older than I was, drove us through the neighborhoods of San Antonio to view Christmas lights so Santa could visit our house. When we returned, we lined up, youngest to oldest, and opened the front door to behold the miracle of Christmas, okay, the Christmas gifts. But, I'm getting ahead of myself. Dinner came before gifts.

Our Christmas Eve meal always featured a shrimp dish in keeping with the meat abstinence rules of the Catholics at the time. I had no appetite for this meal and remember little about it. I doubt I ate much of anything, certainly not the shrimp. I understand now that meals during the holidays are for the adults, not the children. Please the grown-ups, keep it low-key, and success is guaranteed.

Most of this menu is prepared ahead of time, so you'll have more time for last minute wrapping and visiting with your family. The meal is casual, as often my sons and their families are just arriving from their travels and eating times are in flux. The Mexican soup is easy to keep warm, and I harken back to my San Antonio roots by serving local tamales alongside the soup. An assortment of cheeses and crackers serve as appetizers and provide a hand-held option, so everyone can roam about and interact.

Fortune smiled on me when a work assignment led me to the vibrant city of Barcelona, Spain. My visits there were brief but long enough for me to embrace the casual food scene. My favorite dinner spot was a local tapas bar.

Part bar, part restaurant, tapas bars dotted almost every block of the bustling city. Even though my favorite spot was crowded, even early in the evening, I always managed to locate a vacant stool at the bar. Here was front row viewing for nonstop sangria production. Handsome Spanish bartenders theatrically raised bottles high in the air while streaming alcohol and orange juice effortlessly into crystal pitchers below. Taking notes on my iPhone, I jotted down the ingredients of this delicious sangria, hoping to one day recreate the magic. It's the best!

BARCELONA SANGRIA

MAKES about 6 servings

3 cups dry red wine

3 cups fresh orange juice or from concentrate

3 ounces gin

3 ounces orange liqueur

3 ounces brandy

1½ cups 7UP or ginger ale

Orange slices, for garnish (optional)

1. In a medium to large pitcher, mix together the red wine, orange juice, gin, orange liqueur, brandy, and 7UP. Float a slice or two of orange on top (if using).

2. Serve in a tall glass over ice.

Three cups of wine is almost a full bottle, don't hesitate to use the entire bottle in this recipe without adjusting any of the other ingredients. To make a small pitcher, reduce the amounts by one third.

I've adapted this soup recipe from a Jill Cole recipe originally printed in December 2000 in Bon Appétit. *For many years, I browned the meatballs prior to poaching them but discovered through trial and error that they are far more tender when simply simmered in the broth. As with so many soups, while good the day it's made, it's even better the day after.*

MEXICAN-STYLE MEATBALL SOUP

SERVES 8

Broth

2 tablespoons extra-virgin olive oil
1 large onion, coarsely chopped
2 bay leaves
2 garlic cloves, minced
½ teaspoon chili powder
½ teaspoon smoked paprika
5 (14½-ounce) cans beef broth
1 (28-ounce) can diced tomatoes, with juices
½ cup medium-hot tomato salsa
¼ cup chopped fresh cilantro
½ teaspoon kosher salt
¼ teaspoon ground black pepper

Meatballs

1 pound lean ground beef
¼ pound pork sausage
6 tablespoons yellow cornmeal
¼ cup whole milk
1 large egg
½ teaspoon kosher salt
½ teaspoon ground black pepper
½ teaspoon ground cumin
1 cup finely chopped onion
2 garlic cloves, minced
¼ cup chopped fresh cilantro

Finishing

½ cup long-grain white rice
1 lime, for squeezing

Broth

1. Heat the oil in a large heavy pot over medium-high heat until the oil is shimmering. Add the onions and bay leaves. Reduce the heat to medium and sauté until soft, about 5 minutes. Add the garlic, chili powder, and paprika; heat until fragrant, about 30 seconds.

2. Add the broth, tomatoes with juices, salsa, cilantro, salt, and pepper; bring to a boil, then reduce the heat to low, cover, and simmer for 20 minutes.

Meatballs

1. While the broth is simmering, in a medium bowl, combine the ground beef, pork sausage, cornmeal, milk, egg, salt, pepper, cumin, onion, garlic and cilantro.

Mix well with your hands, using a light touch so the meat is not crushed. Shape mixture into 1- to 1½-inch bite-size balls.

Finishing

1. After the broth simmers, add the rice and meatballs to the soup and bring to a boil, stirring occasionally.

2. Reduce the heat to low, cover, and simmer until the rice and meatballs are tender, about 20 minutes, stirring occasionally.

3. Let cool and skim off the fat and remove the bay leaves. Taste and add more salt and pepper if needed. Finish with a squeeze of fresh lime juice.

This simple salad of buttery Bibb lettuce is layered with sliced oranges and sprinkled with finely chopped red onion and shaved Parmigiano-Reggiano. If Bibb lettuce is not available, any tender mild lettuce works well.

BIBB LETTUCE AND ORANGE SALAD

SERVES 4 to 6

1 teaspoon Dijon mustard
1 tablespoon fresh lemon juice
1 tablespoon white wine vinegar
3 tablespoons extra-virgin olive oil
1 teaspoon pomegranate juice extract (optional)
½ teaspoon kosher salt, plus more as needed
½ teaspoon ground black pepper, plus more as needed
4 small oranges
2 heads of Bibb or Boston lettuce
4 tablespoons finely chopped red onion, rinsed in cold water and dried
Shaved Parmigiano-Reggiano, for serving

1. In a large bowl, whisk together the mustard, lemon juice, vinegar, oil, pomgranate extract (if using), salt, and pepper. Taste and adjust the seasonings if needed. Set aside.

2. On a cutting board, with a sharp knife, slice off both ends of the orange. Stand the orange upright on one of the flat ends and, starting at the top of the orange, slice away the peel, making sure you are slicing away the white pith. Work around the orange until you have a naked orange ball with no white pith. Turn the orange on its side and cut ½-inch slices. Repeat with the remaining oranges.

3. Tear the lettuce into large pieces, then add it to the bowl with the dressing and toss lightly.

4. Arrange the lettuce on a large platter. Place the orange slices on top of the lettuce, then add the red onion and Parmigiano-Reggiano

You wont find a better nut pie than this one. Once served at the now defunct Battletown Inn in Berryville, Virginia, the recipe was published by Bon Appétit *in 1999. I've tinkered with this recipe over the years by decreasing the sugar and adding molasses to it. I make it at least once every holiday season, sometimes substituting pecans for the walnuts; both are equally good. I rarely have any leftovers.*

I've lost count on how many different pastry recipes I've tried, finally settling on an adaptation of one from J. Kenji López-Alt of Serious Eats *fame. Partially baking the crust is a little more trouble, but the result is worth it. The keys to success are: don't overwork the crust, chill it well, and make sure your oven is really up to temperature before baking.*

BOURBON WALNUT PIE

SERVES 8 to 10 | EQUIPMENT: food processor, 9-inch pie plate, kitchen shears, pie weights

Crust

1 1/3 cups all-purpose flour (divided)
1 tablespoon granulated sugar
1/2 teaspoon kosher salt
10 tablespoons (1 1/4 sticks) unsalted butter, cold, cut into 1/2-inch pieces
3 tablespoons water

Filling

1 cup dark corn syrup
1/4 cup granulated sugar
2 tablespoons molasses
3 large eggs
2 tablespoons unsalted butter, melted
2 tablespoons bourbon
2 tablespoons all-purpose flour
1 teaspoon vanilla extract
1/4 teaspoon kosher salt
3/4 cup chopped walnuts (3 ounces)
1 cup walnut halves (3 ounces)

Bourbon whipped cream, for serving (optional)

Crust

1. Add 2/3 cup of the flour, the sugar, and salt in a food processor and pulse to blend. Add the butter and pulse just until the mixture comes together into clumps. Add the remaining 2/3 cup of flour and pulse a few times just until the mixture resembles coarse meal. Do not over mix. *Note: To measure the flour, first aerate by stirring the flour with a knife, then dip the measuring cup into the flour and*

level with the knife. Even better, if you have a scale, 1⅓ cups of flour equals 6.25 ounces.

2. Transfer the mixture to a large bowl and sprinkle in the water. With a rubber spatula or your hands, fold and press the dough until it comes together into a ball.

3. Gather the dough and flatten into a 4-inch disk. Wrap the dough in plastic wrap and refrigerate for at least 2 hours. *Note: Dough may be prepared up to 2 days ahead and refrigerated. Let it soften at room temperature for about 20 minutes before rolling out.*

4. After the dough rests, roll it out on to a floured surface to a 14-inch round. Carefully transfer it to a 9-inch pie plate. With kitchen shears or a knife, trim the pastry to 1½ inches past the rim. Fold the overhang onto itself so you have a thick border. Crimp decoratively. Let the pie shell rest, covered, in the refrigerator for 60 minutes or overnight.

5. While the crust is chilling preheat the oven to 375°F.

6. Partially bake the crust by lining with a double layer of aluminum foil, so that the sides are completely covered. Fill with pie weights and bake on a baking sheet on the bottom rack of the oven for 16 minutes.

7. Carefully remove the aluminum foil, prick a few holes around the bottom of the crust with a fork, and return to the oven for another 8 minutes or until the bottom crust is just beginning to brown. *Note: For a fully baked crust bake an additional 7 to 8 minutes, watching for the sides of the crust to have browned.*

Filling

1. Preheat the oven to 350°F.

2. In a large bowl, whisk together the syrup, sugar, molasses, eggs, butter, bourbon, flour, vanilla, and salt. Add in the walnuts. Pour the mixture into the prepared crust and place on a baking sheet in the bottom third of the oven.

3. Bake until the crust is golden and the filling is set in the center when the pie is shaken slightly, about 50 minutes. Check the pie after 40 minutes; if the crust or nuts are already brown, cover the top with aluminum foil to prevent burning. The pie will have risen and separated from the sides of the crust a little. Don't worry, once it cools, the filling falls and settles back into the crust. Cool the pie completely before cutting. Serve with bourbon whipped cream (if using).

To make bourbon whipped cream, beat 1 cup heavy cream, 2 tablespoons of sugar, ¼ teaspoon of vanilla and 1 tablespoon of bourbon in a small bowl until thick.

For me, nothing feels more like the Christmas season than waking up to the smells of molasses, brown sugar, and cinnamon. This recipe, a family specialty, originated with Katherine Fink Wurzbach (1849–1925), my great grandmother. No matter the location, be it Panama, Connecticut, or Vietnam, my mother and the post office ensured her children never missed out. Now my siblings and our children continue the tradition. These are typical German Christmas cookies; with a shelf life of over a month, they can be shared and enjoyed throughout the Christmas season.

With the help of my sister, Fran, the original recipe has been modernized a bit and the proportions cut down by more than half. Instead of rolling out the dough and resting the diamond-cut cookies overnight on the counter as we did when I was a child, we roll them into a log and refrigerate overnight. The cookies are hard and crisp, good for dunking in coffee or for a teething baby. They are also good accompanied by a stout beer. For a softer cookie, slightly underbake them.

OMA'S MOLASSES COOKIES

MAKES 75 cookies

- 1 (12-ounce) bottle Grandma's Molasses (do not substitute)
- 1 cup lightly packed light or dark brown sugar
- 5 cups all-purpose flour (divided)
- 2 teaspoons baking soda
- 6 tablespoons vegetable shortening
- 2 teaspoons baking powder
- 1 teaspoon kosher salt
- 2 teaspoons ground cinnamon
- 1 teaspoon ground cloves
- ¾ teaspoon ground nutmeg
- 2 teaspoons ground ginger
- 1½ teaspoons vanilla extract
- Grated zest of 3 large oranges
- 2 cups chopped pecans, plus more as desired

1. In a large pot over medium-high heat, bring the molasses and sugar to boil.
2. While the mixture heats, in a small bowl, mix together 1 cup of the flour and the baking soda. Set aside.
3. Once boiling, remove the sugar mixture from the heat and mix in the vegetable shortening, baking powder, salt, cinnamon, cloves, nutmeg, ginger, vanilla,

orange zest, and pecans. When all of the vegetable shortening has dissolved, add in the soda and flour mixture.

4. With a heavy wooden spoon, stir in 3 cups of the flour, 1 cup at a time, stirring well after each addition. The dough will be very stiff. (The last cup of flour is worked into the dough by hand.)

5. Cover a work surface with wax paper and sprinkle some of the remaining flour over it. Empty about a third of the sticky dough out on to the counter and sprinkle a little flour on top. Knead in enough flour so the dough is stiff but still rollable. Roll the dough into a 1½-inch-wide log shape and wrap in plastic. Continue with the remaining two-thirds of the dough, in two batches. You may not use the entire cup of flour. Refrigerate the three dough logs overnight.

6. The next morning, preheat the oven to 325°F. Line two baking sheets with parchment paper.

7. Remove the chilled dough from the refrigerator and slice each log into ½-inch-thick cookies. Place on the prepared baking sheets, spaced 2 inches apart. Bake for 9 to 10 minutes, watching the first batch carefully to know exactly how long to bake. I often cook a test cookie to make sure of the time, as oven temperatures vary widely, and if you are baking two sheets at a time, you may need to swap the sheets midway through cooking. The cookies should be soft when you remove them from the oven and look a little underdone. Let them cool on the baking sheet for 5 minutes, then move them to a wire rack to cool completely.

Baked cookies can be stored in a tin for a month.

Americano Cocktail

Italian Skewers

Pear and Walnut Salad

Boeuf Bourguignon

Parslied Potatoes

Green Peas with Parmesan

Almond Cream Pie
or
Amaretto Cream Cake with Raspberry Filling

Make Ahead
Up to a month ahead: Bake and freeze the cake.
Up to 2 days ahead: Make the raspberry filling for the cake.
Day before: Make the Boeuf Bourguignon, prepare the unbaked pie crust, candy the walnuts.
Morning of: Make the salad dressing, prep the lettuce, bake the pie crust and prepare the pie or make the frosting and ice the cake.
Afternoon of: Construct the skewers.
Last hour: Plate the salad, prepare the potatoes and the green peas, heat the Boeuf Bourguignon.

NEW YEAR'S EVE

New Year's Eve is the one night of the year when we abandon our early to bed rituals, throw caution to the wind, and celebrate with a night of revelry. While the Christmas meal is usually for family, New Year's Eve is an opportunity for an elegant meal shared with friends, old and new. One of the challenges of the evening is to stay engaged until midnight, so begin the evening a little later than usual, serve the meal in leisurely courses, and keep the aperitifs on the light side.

This menu reflects the melding of international flavors, starting in Italy, moving to France, and finishing with either an all-American pie or an extravagant Italian-inspired cake.

Wild Turkey Kitchen

This simple aperitif tends toward bitter and is not overly strong, perfect to start a long evening of celebration. It was the drink ordered by James Bond in the first of Ian Fleming's novels, giving the evening a sophistication without tuxedos.

AMERICANO COCKTAIL

SERVES 1 | EQUIPMENT: rocks glass

1½ ounces Campari

1½ ounces sweet vermouth

3 ounces chilled club soda or seltzer water, or enough to top off your glass

Lemon twist or orange slice, for garnish

1. Pour the Campari and vermouth into a rocks glass filled with ice. Top with soda, stir, and garnish with a lemon twist or an orange slice.

This simple no-bake appetizer comes via my friend Tina Wright, an inventive cook in her own right. Modify this recipe based on your own tastes. If you can't find the mini red and yellow sweet peppers, substitute full-size bell peppers and use any kind of mild to spicy salami for the meat option. For the vegetarian crowd, substitute artichoke hearts or cherry tomatoes for the soppressata.

ITALIAN SKEWERS

MAKES about 22 | EQUIPMENT: 4½- to 5-inch bamboo picks

- 1 (7-ounce) jar of blue cheese–stuffed olives
- 1 (12-ounce) package mini red and yellow sweet peppers, sliced into 1-inch squares
- 6 ounces Gouda cheese and/or aged cheddar, cut into ½-inch cubes
- 3 ounces sliced soppressata, folded
- 1 (5.75-ounce) jar whole pitted Kalamata olives

1 On each skewer, place a stuffed olive, piece of red pepper, cube of cheese, soppressata, piece of yellow pepper, and a Kalamata olive. Serve.

I use all of the stuffed olives and usually have some leftovers of the cheese, peppers, and Kalamata olives.

A simple green salad is a nice accompaniment to the richness of the beef. The walnuts and the pear add a hint of sweetness to the meal.

PEAR AND WALNUT SALAD

SERVES 6

Walnuts
½ cup walnuts, chopped
1 tablespoon unsalted butter
1 tablespoon light brown sugar
⅛ teaspoon sea salt

Dressing
⅓ cup extra-virgin olive oil
2½ tablespoons apple cider vinegar
1 tablespoon honey
1 teaspoon Dijon mustard
1½ tablespoons finely chopped shallot, rinsed
½ teaspoon kosher salt
¼ teaspoon ground black pepper

Salad
1 large head lettuce of choice or bag of mixed greens
2 pears, chopped into ½-inch cubes
⅓ cup dried sweetened cranberries
2 ounces Parmesan cheese, grated

Walnuts
1. Combine the walnuts, butter, brown sugar, and salt in a small saucepan over medium heat and cook for about 2 minutes, until the butter has melted and the sugar mixture lightly coats the walnuts. Set aside while preparing the dressing. *Note: Can be prepared the day before and stored in an airtight container at room temperature.*

Dressing
1. In a small bowl, whisk together the oil, vinegar, honey, mustard, shallot, salt, and pepper.

Salad
1. In a large bowl, combine the lettuce, pears, and cranberries. Gently toss in the dressing, a little at a time. Continue adding the dressing until the lettuce is lightly covered.
2. Divide the salad onto six salad plates and garnish each with the Parmesan cheese and candied walnuts.

This elegant stew has its roots in Julia Child's Mastering the Art of French Cooking. *It's best prepared the day before, both for maximum flavor and to preserve your sanity. Even though I've simplified the original recipe somewhat, it's still a labor of love. Follow Julie's techniques for braising onions and sautéing mushrooms, and you'll gain a new appreciation for these earthy vegetables. I admit, in a pinch, when small boiling onions are not available, I use frozen ones with excellent results.*

Be particular about your ingredients. Not all roasts are created equal; I prefer using a rump roast, though a chuck roast could be substituted. The rump has a little less fat, which makes the cubing easier. When choosing the red wine for this recipe, always pick something you enjoy drinking, for the flavor is pronounced. Turn on your favorite tunes, sip the last of the red wine, and enjoy an afternoon of cooking.

BOEUF BOURGUIGNON

SERVES 6 to 8 | EQUIPMENT: cheesecloth

Stew

6 bacon slices, cut into 1-inch pieces

1 tablespoon extra-virgin olive oil

3 pounds rump roast, cut into 2-inch cubes and dried

1 large carrot, cut into ¼-inch slices

1 medium onion, sliced

1 teaspoon kosher salt

¼ teaspoon ground black pepper

2 tablespoons all-purpose flour

3 cups full-bodied red wine such as Chianti, Beaujolais, or Burgundy

2 to 3 cups beef stock

1 tablespoon tomato paste

2 cloves garlic, smashed and diced

½ teaspoon dried thyme

1 bay leaf, crumbled

Onions

18 to 24 small onions (1 inch in diameter)

1½ tablespoons unsalted butter

1½ tablespoons extra-virgin olive oil

4 parsley sprigs

½ bay leaf

2 thyme sprigs or ¼ teaspoon dried thyme leaves

½ cup beef stock or dry white wine, red wine, or water

Mushrooms

4 tablespoons unsalted butter

2 tablespoons extra-virgin olive oil

1 pound fresh mushrooms

Recipe continued on next page

Stew

1. Preheat the oven to 325°F.

2. In a heatproof lidded 10-inch pan, 3 inches deep, over medium heat, cook the bacon in the oil until the fat is rendered and the bacon is lightly browned, 3 to 4 minutes. Transfer the bacon to a side dish.

3. Increase the heat to medium-high and when the fat is almost smoking, add the beef and cook until browned on all sides. Do this in batches so as not to overcrowd the beef. Set aside the beef with the bacon. In the same pan with the fat, add the carrot and onion and cook until softened, about 5 minutes. Transfer the carrot and onion to the side dish and discard the fat from the pan.

4. Return the meat and vegetable mixture back to the pan and toss with the salt and pepper. Sprinkle the flour over the meat. On medium-high heat, brown the flour while stirring the meat, about 2 minutes. Stir in the wine and enough beef stock so the meat is barely covered. Add the tomato paste, garlic, thyme, and bay leaf. Bring to a simmer, then cover the pan and set it in the lower third of the oven.

5. Slowly simmer the beef in the oven for 3 to 4 hours. Check on the stew periodically and lower the oven temperature if the liquid is boiling rather than simmering. I often reduce the heat to 300°F. When the meat is easily pierced with a fork, it is ready.

Onions

1. While the meat is cooking or even earlier in the day, prepare the onions and the mushrooms. Peel the onions by dropping them into a pot of boiling water for 5 to 10 seconds. Drain, then run cold water over them. Trim off the top and bottom of the onions and carefully slip off just the outer layer of skin. Pierce a cross in the root ends to ensure even cooking. This is not necessary if you are using tiny pearl onions. Dry the onions.

2. Melt the butter and oil in a large skillet over medium heat until the butter foams. Add the onions and sauté, gently stirring with a spatula, until lightly browned, 5 to 8 minutes.

3. Prepare the herb bouquet by tying together in a small piece of cheesecloth the parsley, bay leaf, and thyme.

4. Add the beef stock and herb bouquet to the skillet, cover, and simmer for 30 to 40 minutes, until the onions are tender but retain their shape and the liquid has evaporated. Remove the herb bouquet.

Mushrooms

1. In a large skillet over high heat, melt 2 tablespoons of the butter and mix with 1 tablespoon of the oil. Watch carefully for the butter to foam; as soon as you

see the foam begin to subside (indicating the pan is hot enough), add half of the mushrooms.

2. Toss and shake the mushrooms for 4 to 5 minutes. At first the mushrooms will absorb the oil, but in 2 to 3 minutes, the fat will reappear and the mushrooms will start to brown. Remove from the heat immediately. Repeat this process with the remaining oil, butter, and mushrooms.

The secret to successfully sautéed and browned mushrooms is to start with perfectly dry mushrooms and very hot butter. You must not crowd them or they steam and become soggy. For a pound of mushrooms you will likely need to make two batches, dividing the oil and butter accordingly.

Finishing the Stew

1. When the meat is tender, separate the meat mixture from the sauce by setting a colander over a medium saucepan and carefully pouring the meat mixture into the colander while the liquid empties into the saucepan.

2. Rinse out the 10-inch pan, return the meat mixture to it, and add the cooked onions and mushrooms.

3. In the saucepan, skim off any fat. Bring the sauce to a simmer over medium-low heat and cook for a few minutes, continuing to skim off any fat. You should have at least 2½ cups of sauce that is thick enough to very lightly coat a spoon. If it is too thin, boil it down rapidly or, if it is too thick, add some stock. Taste carefully and adjust the seasoning if needed. *Note: I always have to boil it down.*

4. Pour the sauce over the meat and vegetables and, if serving immediately, cover the pan and simmer for 2 to 3 minutes, basting the meat with the sauce. If making ahead of time, cover and refrigerate.

5. To serve, arrange the stew on a platter surrounded by the Parslied Potatoes.

Boiled potatoes are traditionally served with boeuf bourguignon, but rice or noodles are good substitutes. Paramount to the success of this dish are evenly sized potatoes. I often cut my red potatoes in half if they are unusually large.

PARSLIED POTATOES

SERVES 4 to 6

2 pounds small red potatoes, unpeeled and halved if larger than a golf ball

2 teaspoons kosher salt

2 tablespoons unsalted butter

2 tablespoons roughly chopped parsley

Ground black pepper

1. Put the potatoes and salt into a large pot and cover with 2 inches of water. Bring to a boil, then reduce the heat to low and simmer for 7 minutes. Check to see if the potatoes are tender. The potatoes will take between 7 and 12 minutes to cook, depending on the size.

2. Drain the potatoes in a colander, return them to the pot, then add the butter, parsley, and pepper. Taste for seasonings.

Peas are a perfect green accompaniment to the hardy stew. A simple way to enliven frozen peas is with the addition of shallots and Parmesan cheese.

GREEN PEAS WITH PARMESAN

SERVES 6

2 tablespoons unsalted butter
3 small shallots, sliced
1 (14-ounce) bag frozen peas, thawed
Kosher salt
½ teaspoon fresh lemon juice
¼ cup grated Parmesan cheese
Ground black pepper

1. In a large skillet over medium heat, melt the butter. Add the shallots and sauté until soft, about 3 minutes. Stir in the peas and a few pinches of salt. Cook for 2 to 3 minutes, until warmed through.

2. Remove from the heat, then stir in the lemon juice. Pour into a serving dish and finish by sprinkling in the Parmesan cheese and black pepper.

Wild Turkey Kitchen

For many years, this pie was my signature dessert, served to all first-time dinner guests.

ALMOND CREAM PIE

SERVES 6 to 8 | EQUIPMENT: 9-inch pie plate, electric mixer

- 3 large egg yolks
- ¾ cup plus 6 tablespoons granulated sugar (divided)
- 3 tablespoons cornstarch
- ¼ teaspoon kosher salt
- 2 cups whole or 2% milk
- 2 tablespoons unsalted butter, room temperature
- 1 teaspoon almond extract (divided)
- 3 egg whites, room temperature
- ¼ teaspoon cream of tartar
- 1 (9-inch) baked pastry shell (see page 138 for fully cooked single crust recipe)
- ½ cup sliced almonds

1. In a medium heatproof bowl, lightly beat the egg yolks with a fork. Set aside.

2. Combine ¾ cup of the sugar, cornstarch, and salt in a medium saucepan. Place over medium heat and gradually stir in the milk. Continue to stir until the mixture boils and thickens, 2 to 3 minutes. Once the mixture boils, heat for 2 minutes longer.

3. Remove from the heat and stir a few tablespoons of the hot mixture into the egg yolks. While continuing to stir, slowly add about a quarter of the hot mixture into the eggs. Pour the now warm eggs back into the pan.

4. Place the pan back over medium heat and continue to whisk. Cook for 2 minutes more. The filling will be thick and smooth.

5. Remove from the heat and add the butter and ½ teaspoon of the almond extract. Cover the mixture with plastic wrap or wax paper, ensuring that the wrap touches the top of the mixture. (This prevents a crust from forming.)

6. Meanwhile, make the meringue. Preheat the oven to 350°F.

7. In a large bowl using an electric mixer, beat the egg whites with the cream of tartar and remaining ½ teaspoon of almond extract until soft peaks form.

8. Gradually add the remaining 6 tablespoons of sugar, beating until stiff peaks form and all of the sugar is dissolved.

9. Pour the cooled custard into the baked shell and spread the meringue over the pie, making sure the meringue seals the sides of the pie.

10 Cover the meringue with the sliced almonds.

11 Bake the pie on a baking sheet in the bottom third of the oven for 12 to 15 minutes, or until the meringue is golden. Watch carefully.

12 Refrigerate the pie and serve after it is thoroughly chilled.

This cake is a beautiful, somewhat extravagant cake befitting New Year's or any special occasion. Sandwiched between the three layers is a tart raspberry filling topped with an amaretto cream cheese frosting. The cake takes a bit of time to prepare but holds up well to freezing, so it's a perfect make-ahead recipe, with or without the raspberry filling.

AMARETTO CREAM CAKE WITH RASPBERRY FILLING

SERVES 12 | EQUIPMENT: 3 (9-inch) round cake pans, electric mixer

- 2 teaspoons baking soda
- 1 cup buttermilk
- ½ cup amaretto liqueur
- 1 cup (2 sticks) unsalted butter, room temperature
- 2½ cups granulated sugar (divided)
- ½ teaspoon kosher salt
- ½ teaspoon baking powder
- 1 teaspoon vanilla extract
- 1 teaspoon coconut extract
- 5 large eggs, separated and room temperature
- 3 cups all-purpose flour, plus more for dusting
- 1 cup sweetened shredded coconut
- 1 cup chopped pecans, toasted (see note on page 41)
- Italian Cream Cheese Frosting (recipe follows)
- Raspberry Filling (recipe follows)

1. Preheat the oven to 325°F. Grease 3 (9-inch) pans with pan spray or butter and dust with flour. Line the bottom of each pan with parchment paper.

2. In a small bowl, stir together the baking soda and buttermilk, then mix in the amaretto. Set aside.

3. In the bowl of a stand mixer fitted with the paddle attachment, or in a large bowl using a hand-held mixer, cream together the butter, 2 cups of sugar, salt, baking powder, vanilla, and coconut extract until light and fluffy, 3 to 4 minutes. Add in the egg yolks, one at a time, taking care to mix well after each yolk. Reduce the mixer speed to low and sprinkle in a third of the flour. Lightly mix. Add in half of the buttermilk mixture and combine. Continue in this manner, alternating between flour and buttermilk, ending with the flour. Set aside.

4. In a separate large bowl, beat the egg whites with an electric mixer until soft peaks just begin to form. Slowly add the remaining ½ cup of sugar and whip to stiff peaks.

5. Carefully combine the egg whites with the batter by adding a dollop of egg whites to the batter and lightly mixing with a rubber spatula to lighten the mixture. Place another dollop of egg whites in the batter, this time with a spatula, carefully cutting down the middle of the bowl, then up the sides and over. Rotate the bowl a quarter of a turn. Once no pockets of egg whites remain, continue with another spoonful. Repeat until the egg whites are very lightly incorporated into the batter.

6. Fold in the coconut and pecans. The batter will be very thick. Divide into the prepared pans and smooth the batter. Bake until a tester inserted in the center comes out clean, 30 to 35 minutes, watching carefully.

7. Remove from the oven and cool in the pans for 10 minutes, then remove from the pans and cool completely on wire racks.

8. To frost the cake, place the bottom layer on a serving plate and cover with a thin layer of frosting, then top with half of the raspberry filling. Repeat with the second cake layer, frosting, and the remaining half of filling. Top with the third layer, then cover the cake with the remaining frosting. Depending on how heavily you coat the cake, you may have frosting left over.

This cake can be prepared up to one day ahead. Cover in plastic wrap. The cake layers can also be made up to a month ahead of time, wrapped tightly, and frozen.

Italian Cream Cheese Frosting

The almond flavors from the amaretto liqueur in this frosting add another level of decadence to an already special dessert.

MAKES enough to fill and frost 3 (9-inch) layers | EQUIPMENT: electric mixer

¾ cup (1½ sticks) unsalted butter, room temperature

1 (12-ounce) package cream cheese, room temperature

¼ cup amaretto liqueur

1 teaspoon vanilla extract

1 (16-ounce) box powdered sugar, sifted

1. In the bowl of a stand mixer fitted with the paddle attachment, or in a large bowl if using a hand-held mixer, cream together the butter and cream cheese until fluffy, 3 to 5 minutes. Beat in the amaretto and vanilla.

2. Gradually beat in the powdered sugar until smooth.

Raspberry Filling

This simple tart raspberry filling holds up well to the sweet cream cheese frosting. Make sure both the cake and the filling are completely cool before using. If you prefer a seedless filling, pass the mixture through a metal strainer before cooling.

MAKES 1½ cups

3 tablespoons granulated sugar

3 tablespoons cornstarch

3 tablespoons water

1 (12-ounce) package frozen raspberries

1 teaspoon fresh lemon juice

1. In a medium saucepan combine the sugar and cornstarch. Add in the water and mix over low heat, stirring until there are no lumps.
2. Add the raspberries and turn the heat to medium. While stirring, bring the raspberry mixture to a boil and cook for another minute. Remove from the heat, add the lemon juice, then cool completely before using.

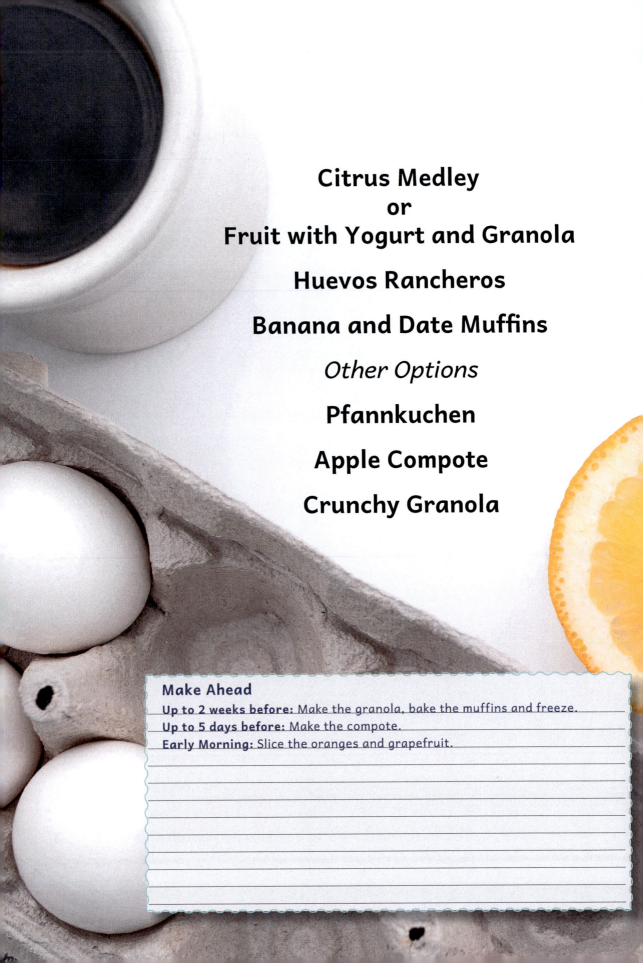

**Citrus Medley
or
Fruit with Yogurt and Granola**

Huevos Rancheros

Banana and Date Muffins

Other Options

Pfannkuchen

Apple Compote

Crunchy Granola

Make Ahead
Up to 2 weeks before: Make the granola, bake the muffins and freeze.
Up to 5 days before: Make the compote.
Early Morning: Slice the oranges and grapefruit.

BREAKFAST WITH FRIENDS

One of my favorite times for a leisurely meal is the morning after a party when friends stay over for the night. Conversation is relaxed and the coffee is strong. Many of these dishes are simple, and I often improvise on the spot using the staples in my refrigerator. Fresh fruit is always a component. This is not a traditional menu but a potpourri of breakfast dishes that can be made alone or mixed and matched.

This isn't so much a recipe as it is an arrangement of seasonally available fruit with citrus as its backbone.

CITRUS MEDLEY

SERVES 4

1 large grapefruit
3 small oranges
1 pint strawberries, sliced

Pinch sea salt
Mint, parsley, or rosemary sprigs, for garnish

1. With a sharp knife, slice off both ends of the grapefruit. Next, slide the knife along the edge of the peel, exposing the flesh and pulling it away as you move around the fruit. Take off strips of the peel as you go.

2. Cut off any pith (bitter white part) that you missed.

3. Cut the grapefruit into sections by sliding your knife along the inside of the membrane of each section. Pop out each section and then move on to the next. Set aside.

4. With a sharp knife, slice off the ends of an orange. Stand the orange upright on one of the flat ends. Starting at the top of each orange, slice away the peel all of the way to the bottom of the cutting board, making sure you are slicing away the white pith. Work around the orange until you have a naked orange ball with little white pith. Turn the orange on its side and cut into ½-inch-thick slices. Repeat with the remaining two oranges.

5. Alternate layers of the orange slices, grapefruit sections, and strawberries on a small plate. Sprinkle the grapefruit with the sea salt. Garnish with a sprig of greenery and serve.

Use any assortment of fruit that is in season. On the morning of the breakfast, I choose two or three fruits that I have on hand. The granola is used as a garnish so any store bought granola is fine, but I've also included one of my favorite granola recipes in this book, so if you happen to have it in your pantry, all the better.

I serve this in one of two ways: either as a parfait with the yogurt layered in the dish or served à la carte with the yogurt spooned over individually.

FRUIT WITH YOGURT AND GRANOLA

SERVES 4

4 tablespoons honey
2 cups low- or full-fat plain Greek yogurt

Assorted fruits in season such as mixed berries and bananas, sliced
Granola, for garnish

For Parfait

1. In a small bowl, mix the honey with the yogurt. Add more honey if you prefer a sweeter yogurt.
2. In four glass parfait or wine glasses, alternate layers of yogurt and fruit.
3. Top each serving with a tablespoon of granola.

For à la Carte

1. Mix the honey with yogurt and serve in a small bowl on the side.
2. Mix the fruit in a medium bowl and top with a sprinkling of granola.

Tomatoes, onions, peppers, and tortillas are the foundation of Mexican-style eggs. Variations to this dish are as varied as the seasons. This recipe relies on canned tomatoes and salsa (jarred or homemade), making it quick to prepare while entertaining friends. Spicy or mild, it's your choice.

HUEVOS RANCHEROS

SERVES 4 to 6

3 tablespoons vegetable oil (divided)
½ cup chopped onion
1 garlic clove, chopped
1 (14½-ounce) can fire-roasted diced tomatoes)
½ cup medium or hot salsa
¼ teaspoon kosher salt, plus more as needed

6 corn tortillas, cut into 1-inch dice
2 teaspoons water
8 large eggs
2 tablespoons unsalted butter
Mexican cheese such as Cotija
Hot sauce, for serving

1. Heat 1 tablespoon of the oil over medium heat in a medium saucepan until shimmering. Add the onion and garlic and sauté until soft. Stir in the tomatoes, salsa, and salt. Taste and add additional salt as needed. Turn the heat to low and let simmer while preparing the tortillas and eggs.

2. In a 10-inch sauté pan or skillet, heat the remaining 2 tablespoons of oil until shimmering, then add the tortillas and heat until the tortillas are starting to crisp. Remove the tortillas to a serving plate, sprinkle with salt, and cover while you prepare the eggs.

3. In a small bowl, whisk together the water and the eggs.

4. Wipe the sauté pan to remove any tortilla crumbs, then add the butter and melt over low heat. If the pan is very hot, remove from the heat for a few seconds so it cools a bit. Add the eggs and cook slowly while gently stirring until just barely done. The eggs come together quickly in the hot pan.

5. To serve, pour the eggs over the tortillas, then top with the warm tomato sauce. Sprinkle with the Mexican cheese and serve extra hot sauce on the side.

A savory accompaniment to the huevos rancheros is a small plate of sliced avocados and fresh tomatoes. Sprinkle with salt and pepper and drizzle lemon over the avocado slices.

I received this recipe from Elizabeth San Marco, one of my oldest and dearest friends. Once while visiting her, she offered me a muffin with the caveat that they were supposedly very healthy, no sugar, no gluten. Suspicious yet trusting, I ate one, then asked for another, and then more to eat on my trip home. They are extremely moist, almost wet, and not too sweet. Now I keep a stash of these in my freezer, ready for the most discerning overnight guest.

I suggest making these ahead of time and defrosting them the night before your breakfast or microwaving them straight from the freezer.

BANANA AND DATE MUFFINS

MAKES 12 muffins | EQUIPMENT: muffin pan, cupcake liners, food processor

2 cups almond flour
2 teaspoons baking soda
½ teaspoon sea salt
1 tablespoon ground cinnamon
1 cup dates, chopped
3 medium ripe bananas

3 large eggs
1 teaspoon apple cider vinegar
¼ cup coconut oil, melted
1½ cups grated peeled carrots
¾ cup finely chopped walnuts (or nut of choice)

1. Preheat the oven to 350°F. Line a muffin pan with cupcake liners.
2. In a large bowl, combine the almond flour, baking soda, salt, and cinnamon. Set aside.
3. In a food processor, mix together the dates, bananas, eggs, vinegar, and coconut oil until the dates and bananas are well chopped.
4. Add the date mixture to the flour mixture and combine thoroughly. Fold in the carrots and the nuts.
5. Spoon the mixture into the prepared pan and bake for 25 minutes. Cool to room temperature and freeze in plastic bags or eat right away.

This family recipe originated with my great grandmother, Katherine Fink Wurzbach. Having never known her, the thread of our connection is these pancakes. Of German heritage, she was mother to nine children, four boys and five girls. Two of the boys were prominent congressmen from San Antonio and one of the girls was my grandmother, Lily.

My mother prepared these often, sans recipe. My sister Fran penned the recipe, which was pivotal in preserving the dish's unique characteristics. Pfannkuchens are essentially a German variation of the French crepe, but they are thinner and slightly crunchy when made correctly. Serve them with butter and syrup and rolled up like a cigar. For a fancier presentation, add a side of salty bacon and an apple compote to the plate.

The downside to these is that they are best eaten right off the stove, relegating the host to somewhat of a short-order cook. Family lore holds that the Wurzbach family of eleven served these on weekends and couldn't keep a cook employed after one round of pfannkuchens.

PFANNKUCHEN

MAKES 5 to 6

1 large egg
⅓ cup all-purpose flour
½ cup whole or 2% milk
Pinch kosher salt

Vegetable oil
Unsalted butter, for serving
Syrup, for serving

1. In a medium bowl, beat the egg with a fork, then add the flour, milk, and salt. Use a fork to whisk until relatively smooth. There will still be a few lumps. Let the mixture rest for at least 5 minutes.

2. Heat about a teaspoon of oil in an 8-inch skillet over medium heat until shimmering. Add less than ¼ cup of the batter to the pan and swirl to lightly cover the bottom of the pan completely. Cook on one side until brown around the edges, about 2 minutes, then flip and cook on the other side for less than a minute. If using a nonstick skillet, simply rub the pan with an oil-moistened paper towel before starting the next pfannkuchen. You may need more oil, depending on your pan.

3. To serve, lightly cover the crepe with butter and syrup. Roll up cigar style.

The tartness of these apples compliments many sweet breakfast dishes and is a natural paring for bacon or sausage.

APPLE COMPOTE

SERVES 4

- 2 to 3 tart apples, peeled or unpeeled, cored, and cut into chunks (about 1 pound)
- 1 tablespoon water
- 2 tablespoons granulated sugar
- 1 teaspoon fresh lemon juice
- Spices as desired (cinnamon, nutmeg, allspice, cloves)
- 1 teaspoon vanilla extract

1. Place the apples, water, sugar, lemon juice, and spices into a small heavy saucepan and stir over medium-high heat until the mixture comes to a boil.

2. Reduce the heat to low, cover, and simmer, stirring occasionally, until the apples have softened, 15 to 20 minutes. Add the vanilla and heat through. Serve warm or cool and store up to 5 days in the refrigerator.

Homemade granola is a rich treat for breakfast. Rather than eating a whole bowl on its own, I use this as a garnish for a serving of bran flakes or for fruit and yogurt. I've adapted this recipe from one I discovered by Jenny Rosenstrach in Bon Appétit *in February 2013. It keeps for a month stored in an airtight container at room temperature. The egg white is the secret to the crunch.*

CRUNCHY GRANOLA

MAKES 2 quarts

1 large egg white

3 cups old-fashioned rolled oats (not instant)

1½ cups chopped nuts (pecans, walnuts or almonds or a mixture)

1½ cups unsweetened coconut flakes

½ cup maple syrup

¼ cup extra-virgin olive oil or coconut oil

¼ cup raw or toasted pumpkin seeds

2 tablespoons light brown sugar

1 teaspoon kosher salt

½ teaspoon ground cinnamon

1 cup dried cranberries or cherries

1. Preheat the oven to 300°F.
2. In a large bowl, mix together egg white, oats, nuts, coconut, syrup, oil, pumpkin seeds, brown sugar, salt, and cinnamon.
3. Spread out the mixture on a rimmed baking sheet and bake until golden brown and dry, stirring every 10 minutes. It takes a total of 40 to 45 minutes. Let cool on the baking sheet. The mixture turns crispy as it cools. When cool, add in the dried cranberries or cherries.

Index

Page references in *italics* indicate photographs.

A

Almond Cream Pie 152, *153*
Amaretto Cream Cake with Raspberry Filling 154, *155*
Americano Cocktail 144
appetizers
    Bacon and Pecan Pimento Cheese 40, *41*
    Candied Bacon Bites 66, *67*
    Cheese Böreks 50, *51*
    Cowboy Caviar *122*, 123
    Deviled Green Eggs and Ham *86*, 87
    Italian Skewers 145
    Mad Hatter Cucumber Tea Sandwiches 85
    Mango Guacamole Dip *42*, 43
    Spanakopita 36, *37*
    Sun-Dried Tomato Dip on Pringles *38*, 39
Apple Compote 168
Asian-Style Tomato Salad 29
Awesome Coconut Cake 62

B

baby lit shower 81
    Cream Cheese Frosting 91
    Deviled Green Eggs and Ham *86*, 87
    Ginger Grapefruit Sparklers 82, *83*
    In the Night Kitchen Bourbon Pecan Cookies *92*, 93
    Mad Hatter Cucumber Tea Sandwiches 85
    Mr. McGregor's Cakes (The World's Best Carrot Cake) 88, *90*
    Peppermint Cranberry Mocktails 82, *83*
    Red Fish, Blue Fish, Tuna Salad 84
backyard grill 95
    Banana Cream Pudding 110, *111*
    Beef Sliders with Sweet and Sour Red Onions 100, *101*
    Charlie Bird's Farro Salad 107
    Chicken Tikka Skewers *102*, 103
    Cucumber Raita 105
    Frozen Lime Pie *108*, 109
    Lemon Jasmine Rice Salad 106
    Marshmallow Meringue 113
    Naan 98, *99*
    Summer Bourbon Rickey 97
    Vanilla Pastry Cream 112
    Watermelon Chaat 104
Bacon and Pecan Pimento Cheese 40, *41*
Banana and Date Muffins *164*, 165
Banana Cream Pudding 110, *111*
Barcelona Sangria 132, *133*
beef
    Beef Sliders with Sweet and Sour Red Onions 100, *101*
    Boeuf Bourguignon 147, *150*
    Bourbon Meatloaf 24, *25*
    Brisket on a Biscuit 116, *117*
    Mexican-Style Meatball Soup 134, *135*
Beef Sliders with Sweet and Sour Red Onions 100, *101*
Bibb Lettuce and Orange Salad 136, *137*
birthday celebration 49
    Awesome Coconut Cake 62
    Cheese Böreks 50, *51*
    Chicken Paprikas 52
    Chocolate Ganache 59
    Coconut Cream Cheese Frosting 63
    Mexican Chocolate Pepita Cake with Candied Ancho Chilies 56, *58*
    Provincial Cherry Tomato Gratin 55
    Raspberry Sauce 60
    Vanilla Custard Sauce 61
    Vegetable Toss 54
Boeuf Bourguignon 147, *150*
book club 115
    Brisket on a Biscuit 116, *117*
    Cowboy Caviar *122*, 123
    Midnight Chocolate Cake with Orange-Lemon Curd Filling 126, *128*
    Mixed Fruit Crisp with Almonds 124, *125*
    Orange-Lemon Curd Filling 127
    Spicy Cold Tomato Soup 120, *121*
    Sugared Pecans 129
    Tomato Bisque 118, *119*
bourbon
    Bourbon Meatloaf 24, *25*
    Bourbon Walnut Pie 138
    Summer Bourbon Rickey 97
    Wild Turkey Lemonade 22, *23*
Bourbon Meatloaf 24, *25*
Bourbon Walnut Pie 138
breakfast & brunch
    Apple Compote 168
    Banana and Date Muffins *164*, 165
    Citrus Medley 160
    Crunchy Granola 169
    Fruit with Yogurt and Granola 161
    Huevos Rancheros 162, *163*

Index

Pfannkuchen 166, *167*
breakfast with friends 159
  Apple Compote 168
  Banana and Date Muffins *164*, 165
  Citrus Medley 160
  Crunchy Granola 169
  Fruit with Yogurt and Granola 161
  Huevos Rancheros 162, *163*
  Pfannkuchen 166, *167*
Brisket on a Biscuit 116, *117*
Bunco party or dinner for twelve 65
  Candied Bacon Bites 66, *67*
  Chicken Vegetable Cobbler *68*, 69
  Dark Chocolate Pudding with Toasted Coconut 78, *79*
  Fresh Tomato and Cucumber Salad 75
  Lemon Cake 76
  Lemon Cream Cheese Glaze 77
  Sweet and Spicy Candied Pecans 74
  Waldorf Salad *72*, 73

C

cakes
  Awesome Coconut Cake 62
  Lemon Cake 76
  Mexican Chocolate Pepita Cake with Candied Ancho Chilies 56, *58*
  Midnight Chocolate Cake with Orange-Lemon Curd Filling 126, *128*
  Mr. McGregor's Cakes (The World's Best Carrot Cake) 88, *90*
Candied Bacon Bites 66, *67*
Charlie Bird's Farro Salad 107
Cheese Böreks 50, *51*
chicken
  Chicken Paprikas 52
  Chicken Tikka Skewers *102*, 103
  Chicken Vegetable Cobbler *68*, 69
Chicken Paprikas 52
Chicken Tikka Skewers *102*, 103
Chicken Vegetable Cobbler *68*, 69
Chocolate Ganache 59
Chocolate-Truffle Cookies *46*, 47
Christmas Eve 131
  Barcelona Sangria 132, *133*
  Bibb Lettuce and Orange Salad 136, *137*
  Bourbon Walnut Pie 138
  Mexican-Style Meatball Soup 134, *135*
  Oma's Molasses Cookies 140, *141*
Citrus Medley 160
Coconut Cream Cheese Frosting 63
cookies
  Chocolate-Truffle Cookies *46*, 47
  Flourless Orange and Almond Cookies 44
  In the Night Kitchen Bourbon Pecan Cookies *92*, 93
  Oma's Molasses Cookies 140, *141*
Cowboy Caviar *122*, 123
Cream Cheese Frosting 91
Crunchy Granola 169
Cucumber Raita 105

D

Dark Chocolate Pudding with Toasted Coconut 78, *79*
desserts
  Almond Cream Pie 152, *153*
  Amaretto Cream Cake with Raspberry Filling 154, *155*
  Awesome Coconut Cake 62
  Banana Cream Pudding 110, *111*
  Bourbon Walnut Pie 138
  Chocolate Ganache 59
  Chocolate-Truffle Cookies *46*, 47
  Coconut Cream Cheese Frosting 63
  Cream Cheese Frosting 91
  Dark Chocolate Pudding with Toasted Coconut 78, *79*
  Flan *32*, 33
  Flourless Orange and Almond Cookies 44
  Frozen Lime Pie *108*, 109
  In the Night Kitchen Bourbon Pecan Cookies *92*, 93
  Italian Cream Cheese Frosting 156
  Lemon Cake 76
  Lemon Cream Cheese Glaze 77
  Marshmallow Meringue 113
  Mexican Chocolate Pepita Cake with Candied Ancho Chilies 56, *58*
  Midnight Chocolate Cake with Orange-Lemon Curd Filling 126, *128*
  Mixed Fruit Crisp with Almonds 124, *125*
  Mr. McGregor's Cakes (The World's Best Carrot Cake) 88, *90*
  Oma's Molasses Cookies 140, *141*
  Orange-Lemon Curd Filling 127
  Raspberry Filling 157
  Raspberry Sauce 60
  Sugared Pecans 129

Index

Vanilla Custard Sauce 61
Vanilla Pastry Cream 112
Deviled Green Eggs and Ham *86*, *87*
drinks
   Americano Cocktail 144
   Barcelona Sangria 132, *133*
   Ginger Grapefruit Sparklers 82, *83*
   Peppermint Cranberry Mocktails 82, *83*
   Summer Bourbon Rickey 97
   Wild Turkey Lemonade 22, *23*

F

Flan *32*, 33
Flourless Orange and Almond Cookies 44
Fresh Tomato and Cucumber Salad 75
frosting
   Chocolate Ganache 59
   Coconut Cream Cheese Frosting 63
   Cream Cheese Frosting 91
   Italian Cream Cheese Frosting 156
   Lemon Cream Cheese Glaze 77
Frozen Lime Pie *108*, 109
Fruit with Yogurt and Granola 161

G

Ginger Grapefruit Sparklers 82, *83*
Green Peas with Parmesan 151

H

Herbed Polenta with Brie *26*, 27
Huevos Rancheros 162, *163*

I

In the Night Kitchen Bourbon Pecan Cookies *92*, 93
Italian Cream Cheese Frosting 156
Italian Skewers 145

L

Lemon Cake 76
Lemon Cream Cheese Glaze 77
Lemon Jasmine Rice Salad 106

M

Mad Hatter Cucumber Tea Sandwiches 85
mains
   Beef Sliders with Sweet and Sour Red Onions 100, *101*
   Boeuf Bourguignon 147, *150*
   Bourbon Meatloaf 24, *25*
   Brisket on a Biscuit 116, *117*
   Chicken Paprikas 52
   Chicken Tikka Skewers *102*, 103
   Chicken Vegetable Cobbler 68, 69
   Mango Guacamole Dip *42*, 43
   Marshmallow Meringue 113
   Mexican Chocolate Pepita Cake with Candied Ancho Chilies 56, *58*
   Mexican-Style Meatball Soup 134, *135*
   Midnight Chocolate Cake with Orange-Lemon Curd Filling 126, *128*
   Mixed Fruit Crisp with Almonds 124, *125*
   Mr. McGregor's Cakes (The World's Best Carrot Cake) 88, *90*

N

Naan 98, *99*
New Year's Eve 143
   Almond Cream Pie 152, *153*
   Amaretto Cream Cake with Raspberry Filling 154, *155*
   Americano Cocktail 144
   Boeuf Bourguignon 147, *150*
   Green Peas with Parmesan 151
   Italian Cream Cheese Frosting 156
   Italian Skewers 145
   Parslied Potatoes 150
   Pear and Walnut Salad 146
   Raspberry Filling 157

O

Oma's Molasses Cookies 140, *141*
Orange-Lemon Curd Filling 127

P

Parslied Potatoes 150
Pear and Walnut Salad 146
Peppermint Cranberry Mocktails 82, *83*
Pfannkuchen 166, *167*
pies
   Almond Cream Pie 152, *153*
   Bourbon Walnut Pie 138
   Frozen Lime Pie *108*, 109
pork
   Bacon and Pecan Pimento Cheese 40, *41*
   Candied Bacon Bites 66, *67*
   Deviled Green Eggs and Ham *86*, *87*
   Italian Skewers 145

Index

Mexican-Style Meatball Soup 134, *135*
Provincial Cherry Tomato Gratin 55

R

Raspberry Filling 157
Raspberry Sauce 60
Red Fish, Blue Fish, Tuna Salad 84
Roasted Potatoes 28

S

salads & sides
  Asian-Style Tomato Salad 29
  Bibb Lettuce and Orange Salad 136, *137*
  Charlie Bird's Farro Salad 107
  Cucumber Raita 105
  Fresh Tomato and Cucumber Salad 75
  Green Peas with Parmesan 151
  Herbed Polenta with Brie *26*, 27
  Lemon Jasmine Rice Salad 106
  Naan 98, *99*
  Parslied Potatoes 150
  Pear and Walnut Salad 146
  Provincial Cherry Tomato Gratin 55
  Red Fish, Blue Fish, Tuna Salad 84
  Roasted Potatoes 28
  Shaved Brussels Sprouts Salad 30, *31*
  Sweet and Spicy Candied Pecans 74
  Vegetable Toss 54
  Waldorf Salad *72*, 73
  Watermelon Chaat 104
Shaved Brussels Sprouts Salad 30, *31*

soups
  Mexican-Style Meatball Soup 134, *135*
  Spicy Cold Tomato Soup 120, *121*
  Tomato Bisque 118, *119*
Spanakopita 36, *37*
Spicy Cold Tomato Soup 120, *121*
Sugared Pecans 129
Summer Bourbon Rickey 97
Sunday dinner 21
  Asian-Style Tomato Salad 29
  Bourbon Meatloaf 24, *25*
  Flan *32*, 33
  Herbed Polenta with Brie *26*, 27
  Roasted Potatoes 28
  Shaved Brussels Sprouts Salad 30, *31*
  Wild Turkey Lemonade 22, *23*
  Sun-Dried Tomato Dip on Pringles *38*, 39
  Sweet and Spicy Candied Pecans 74

T

Tomato Bisque 118, *119*
tomatoes
  Asian-Style Tomato Salad 29
  Charlie Bird's Farro Salad 107
  Cowboy Caviar *122*, 123
  Fresh Tomato and Cucumber Salad 75
  Huevos Rancheros 162, *163*
  Mexican-Style Meatball Soup 134, *135*
  Provincial Cherry Tomato Gratin 55
  Spicy Cold Tomato Soup 120, *121*
  Sun-Dried Tomato Dip on Pringles *38*, 39
  Tomato Bisque 118, *119*

V

Vanilla Custard Sauce 61
Vanilla Pastry Cream 112
Vegetable Toss 54

W

Waldorf Salad *72*, 73
Watermelon Chaat 104
Wild Turkey Lemonade 22, *23*
wine tasting party 35
  Bacon and Pecan Pimento Cheese 40, *41*
  Chocolate-Truffle Cookies *46*, 47
  Flourless Orange and Almond Cookies 44
  Mango Guacamole Dip *42*, 43
  Spanakopita 36, *37*
  Sun-Dried Tomato Dip on Pringles *38*, 39

Made in the USA
Las Vegas, NV
15 December 2021